WHAT READE

Unique and insightful! The stu
deep insights into who God is.
and modern-day stories to illustrate His power, love, and grace. This
study will help you rest in the promises of your Savior as you learn more
about who He is and what He does for you.

Christina Hergenrader, speaker and author of *Inspired by the Holy Spirit: Four Habits for Faithful Living*

Michelle's debut book, *Promised Rest*, was thoughtfully created by
someone who I can tell has read and led many Bible studies. Her writing
draws you into her world in a way that makes the teaching come to life.
But also, this book was designed to be read with others as you grow in
faith and relationship. I love that she is able to weave so many great Bible
stories into a seamless narrative. Thank you, Michelle, for such a great
resource to help us rest in who God is!

Lindsay Hausch, author, blogger, and women's ministry leader

Jesus graciously invites us, "Come to Me, all who labor and are heavy
laden, and I will give you rest" (Matthew 11:28). Michelle Diercks leads
us to respond to that invitation and to receive true rest in the midst of
the ordeals and anxieties of life. This book will guide you to reflect on
God's character as revealed in His names so that you might abide in His
peace. As you read these words, the Spirit of God will bring respite, rest,
and renewal to your anxious spirit.

David Peter, professor of practical theology, Concordia Seminary, St. Louis

Slow down and get to know God better in the pages of *Promised Rest*.
Michelle Diercks guides readers through a study of the names of God—
names that reveal various facets of His character. Rediscover the God
of power in the names *Elohim* and *El Shaddai*. Study the names *Yahweh
Ra'ah* and *Jir'eh* to learn more about the Lord's care for you. Read about
the name *El Roi* and rejoice that the Creator of the universe sees you.
Throughout the book, Michelle's very personal stories of the Lord's care
during critical moments in her life remind us that God is still active and
working today. Careful Bible study aids our understanding of the names
of God. Excellent discussion and reflection questions enhance the study
of His character. Linger in the Word and find peace in God's presence.

Sharla Fritz, author and speaker

In these chaotic days, we all need to be reminded of the rest Christ has promised us. In this resource, Michelle shows the readers over and over again that peace and rest do not come from us or our circumstances but from Christ. *Promised Rest* will be a gift to anyone who uses it.

Katie Koplin, writer and speaker

Promised Rest: Finding Peace in God's Presence is like a warm hug packed with truth and grace from God's heart and delivered by a dear and trusted friend. Wisdom and encouragement fill the pages of this study and are reinforced with beautiful Scripture passages telling of God's promises that calm the soul and refresh the weary heart. Timeless truths and thought-provoking questions allow you to dive deeper into your understanding of who God is and who you are in Him. Michelle's grace-filled approach and comforting words usher you into God's presence, wherein you truly do find His perfect peace.

Carol Fedewa, women's ministry coordinator, Hales Corner Lutheran Church

Promised Rest is a wonderful, descriptive way to bring the Word into our lives. Michelle has a soothing way to say God's Word is truth and show how to understand it. The questions throughout the study are both challenging and engaging—not just about the Bible, but also how it relates to our lives. *Promised Rest* made me feel cherished! It was like being wrapped up in a warm towel at a spa! Thank you for this study of God and for the encouragement in our journey with Him.

Cherie Endrihs, director of Christian education and first vice president, Lutheran Women in Mission, Gulf States District

In a world increasingly filled with chaos and uncertainty, Michelle Diercks' insightful book draws us back to the source of true peace and security—the character of God conveyed through His biblical names. In this work you'll be more participant than passive reader, as Diercks employs multiple interactive educational tools to remind us of biblical promises. Part memoir, part exegetical study, and part devotional reflection, individuals and small groups will be blessed by this timely and engaging resource.

Jeffrey Leininger, university pastor, Concordia University Chicago

Does peace seem elusive amid the chaos, difficulties, and distractions of daily life? Does your weary soul long for rest? In *Promised Rest*, author Michelle Diercks gently guides you to the place where peace is found—to the One who provides real rest. This compelling study examines the names and characteristics of God, serving to draw you closer to Him. Each daily lesson reads devotionally, with a combination of relatable stories, biblical narrative, and applicable Scriptures, leading you to learn more about the One who loves you beyond measure, never leaves your side, and fulfills His promises for you in Christ. You'll find engaging questions, journaling space, visual faith illustrations, and so much more in this outstanding resource. Receive rest in the peace of God's presence.

Deb Burma, speaker, retreat leader, and author of *Joy: A Study of Philippians, Be Still & Know: A Study of Rest and Refuge*, and more.

PROMISED REST

FINDING PEACE IN GOD'S PRESENCE

MICHELLE DIERCKS

CONCORDIA PUBLISHING HOUSE • SAINT LOUIS

DEDICATION

Mom and Dad, thank you for
teaching me to trust Jesus in all things.

Troy, your love, support, and
encouragement helped make this book possible.

Jacob and Matthew, thank you for cheering me on
and loving me through the process of writing this book.

Published by Concordia Publishing House
3558 S. Jefferson Ave., St. Louis, MO 63118-3968
1-800-325-3040 • cph.org

Copyright © 2022 Michelle Diercks

Unless otherwise indicated, Scripture quotations are from the ESV® Bible (The Holy Bible, English Standard Version®), copyright © 2001 by Crossway, a publishing ministry of Good News Publishers. Used by permission. All rights reserved.

Quotations marked *LSB* are from *Lutheran Service Book*, copyright © 2006 Concordia Publishing House. All rights reserved.

Quotations marked *TLSB* are taken from the notes, introductory material, or original articles from *The Lutheran Study Bible* © 2009 by Concordia Publishing House. All rights reserved.

Quotations from *Luther's Small Catechism with Explanation* are copyright © 1986, 2017 Concordia Publishing House. All rights reserved.

Quotations from *Lutheran Bible Companion*, vol. 2, are copyright © 2014 Concordia Publishing House. All rights reserved.

Quotations from *Reading Romans with Luther* are copyright © 2016 R. J. Grunewald, published by Concordia Publishing House. All rights reserved.

Quotation from *Luther's Works* are from the American Edition, vols. 3 and 56, copyright © 1961, 2018, respectively, by Concordia Publishing House. All rights reserved.

Manufactured in the United States of America

1 2 3 4 5 6 7 8 9 10   31 30 29 28 27 26 25 24 23 22

CONTENTS

A Note from the Author   6

Introduction   8

How to Use This Study   11

The Five *Rs* of Reflection and Clinging Closer to God   16

Week 1: Elohim   18

    Day 1: Elohim Calls You by Name   20

    Day 2: When Life Is Uncertain   25

    Day 3: The Presence of Elohim   30

    Day 4: Pour Out Your Heart   33

    Day 5: Red Sea Moments   36

    Week 1 Group Study Questions   39

Week 2: Abba   41

    Day 1: You Are Abba's Beloved Child   43

    Day 2: Abba's Gift of Grace   48

    Day 3: Your Sin Is Removed   52

    Day 4: Nothing Can Separate You from Abba's Love   56

    Day 5: Circumstances You Did Not Choose   60

    Week 2 Group Study Questions   63

Week 3: El Roi   65

    Day 1: Desperate Plans   67

    Day 2: El Roi Sees Your Heartache   72

    Day 3: El Roi Sees Your Tears   76

    Day 4: You Are Never Alone   79

    Day 5: The Shelter of His Presence   83

    Week 3 Group Study Questions   88

Week 4: El Shaddai   **90**

     Day 1: Sustained in Sorrow   92

     Day 2: El Shaddai Is Sufficient   96

     Day 3: Impossible Made Possible   101

     Day 4: Rescued from Bitterness   104

     Day 5: Grace Received Is Powerful   109

     Week 4 Group Study Questions   113

Week 5: Jir'eh   **115**

     Day 1: Shattered Dreams Made New   117

     Day 2: Abraham Walks in Faith   121

     Day 3: God Will Provide   125

     Day 4: Held by God   130

     Day 5: Extravagant Love   134

     Week 5 Group Study Questions   139

Week 6: Shalom   **141**

     Day 1: God's Peace Settles Your Heart   143

     Day 2: Israel's Unfaithfulness and God's Faithfulness   148

     Day 3: The Lord Calls Gideon   153

     Day 4: Jesus Gives Us His Peace   157

     Day 5: When Church Hurts   162

     Week 6 Group Study Questions   166

Week 7: Yahweh Ra'ah   **168**

     Day 1: Jesus, the Good Shepherd Carries You   170

     Day 2: The Good Shepherd Knows You   174

     Day 3: He Restores My Soul   178

Day 4: Lost and Found   182

Day 5: The Shepherd's Voice   186

Week 7 Group Study Questions   190

Week 8: Immanuel   **192**

Day 1: God with Us   194

Day 2: Remember the Promises   199

Day 3: You Never Cry Alone   202

Day 4: When You Feel Weary   205

Day 5: Come and Receive the Gifts of Grace   209

Week 8 Group Study Questions   214

Acknowledgments   **216**

Answers to Discussion Questions   **218**

Appendix: A Note to Leaders   **226**

Endnotes   **228**

A Note from the Author

Welcome, friend. I'm delighted you're here.

Take some time. Find a quiet place and join me. Can you hear the gentle whisper of your Savior saying, "Peace! Be still!" (Mark 4:39)? Peace comes from learning to rest in the character of God. The serenity of our soul comes from Him and His work in our lives. But perhaps you can't disengage from everything you have going on, and His words are difficult to hear over the clamor of an overwhelmed mind and an anxious heart. I understand.

While writing this note, my anxious heart drowned out almost everything except my fear. Peace felt far away, and I couldn't be still.

My teenage son wanted to drive on the interstate. On his own. Without me or his dad.

Worry wove its way through my mind and sent my thoughts spinning. Worst-case scenarios flooded my brain. I searched for ways I could control the situation and protect him. I instructed him to take the back roads—it would be safer.

I needn't have worried, because my son is an excellent driver. Besides, it's not his responsibility to deal with my anxious thoughts. I realized that I was imposing my worry on him rather than letting him develop decision-making skills. I took a deep breath, then relented and let him drive away. As he did, I brought my worries before God in prayer, asking for His protection for my son and help for me.

Lord, how am I going to let go? It feels impossible to me. Please keep him safe.

Every time I try to control a circumstance, I fail to remember the character of God. I lose sight of who He is and who I am as His child. Maybe you are like me and have forgotten you are God's child and what that truly means. Are you struggling with troubles that weigh heavily upon your heart? Does wrestling with your thoughts drag you down a slippery slope of despair? Do you wonder how you can be still when instability unsettles your soul?

You are not alone. We all forget. Life is uncertain, and we all face circumstances beyond our control. Peace seems far away. But the truth is that the Lord is a near, dear Friend who provides for you and for all His children, even new drivers. Peace comes only from Him. We find true peace in the wondrous, powerful Word of God—His message for us and to us. We find true peace in God's gifts to us, the hope and comfort that the Holy Spirit instills in our hearts by His Means of Grace. True peace is from Jesus: "Peace I leave with you; My peace I give to you. Not as the world gives do I give to you. Let not your hearts be troubled, neither let them be afraid" (John 14:27).

Still, no one knows what threatens a peaceful heart as does the parent of a teen who just started driving. Except for God, that is. Our heavenly Father sent His Son out into an ugly, dangerous, and murderous world to bring us peace. That's how much our Lord loves us.

I created this study as a meditation on the various names and characteristics of God to deepen your understanding of Him and your identity as His child. The names of God reveal important aspects of His character as well as how He relates to you—His beloved child—and how He offers the peace we all crave so much.

El Shaddai is your hiding place. In the deepest of sorrows, *Immanuel* is there, covering you with His comfort. When waiting disquiets your soul, *Elohim* holds you close to His heart. As you peer into a future you did not plan, *Yahweh Ra'ah* walks with you. When anxiety threatens an ambush, *Shalom* is the peace of God that soothes your heart. *Jir'eh* is God's light during the darkest hours. In Him, you can hide, and *El Roi* gives you hope in His Word and rest in your *Abba* Father's presence.

What you believe to be true about God changes how you live your life, how you see the world, and how you see yourself as His child. As you journey through this study with me, you can rest in the peace of His presence. God holds you in His capable hands and close to His heart.

> I'm praying for you.
> In God's peace and joy,
> Michelle

INTRODUCTION

Silence and solitude are a strange combination with my mom-mobile. I couldn't remember the last time I ran errands by myself.

Signs of spring blanketed eastern Iowa. Driving home, I turned up the radio and sang along—loud and slightly off-key. A scent of chocolate hung in the air; I had discovered a new candy called Bliss, and it lived up to its name.

After a long winter, joy and hope mingled in this perfect early-spring moment. A smile spread across my face and nestled in my heart as I pulled into the garage. Lighthearted and carefree, I gathered my bags and tucked the candy into my purse to share with my husband, Troy, and the boys.

I burst into the house with one hand rooting around in my purse, trying to reach the tasty morsels of chocolate. I looked up with a twinkle in my eye, excited to share the delicious treasure with my family, but it faded when I saw my husband's face. His eyes held a story I did not want to know. He grabbed my hand to pull me close and steady me.

"Michelle, your dad suffered a heart attack. He is being rushed by ambulance to the hospital in Duluth."

My mind roiled with questions. Our sons stood wide-eyed and watching, and their eyes shimmered with unshed tears. They tried to make sense of what had happened to Grandpa. *How bad was he? Would he be okay?*

I searched for a way to fix all that felt wrong, bending the circumstances to my will. My heart ached and my knees weakened as I realized there was nothing I could do. All I wanted was to be with my dad. In that moment, life felt unsettled and wobbly, but amid the turmoil I remembered we would be secure in the peace of God's presence. The promises I remembered from His Word bolstered me.

For God alone my soul waits in silence; from Him comes my
salvation. He alone is my rock and my salvation, my fortress;
I shall not be greatly shaken. (Psalm 62:1–2)

Even as an adult with children of my own, I longed for Dad's safe embrace and assurances that everything would be okay. As I thought about him, one of his favorite phrases came to mind: "You can trust God." I hugged Troy and my boys close. We prayed that the Lord would hold my dad in His capable hands. And peace covered us.

Life catches all of us off guard. Kids have car accidents. Parents get sick. Bad things happen. But our God holds us close to His heart. Even in the very worst situations, we can be still and know that He is God. He is with us. He is our constant companion and very real help in the time of trouble. Active, intimate, and merciful, the God of all comfort is present.

The way we see and remember God changes our view of life and how we live it. When we are certain of His peace and presence, we can endure the bad things and rejoice in the good things.

The peace of God's presence gives us hope in uncertainty, strength for each moment, and the ability to persevere through trials. His presence provides a place for our souls to rest in who He is as our loving Creator.

How do we know God is present with us? We know because of what we see—the earth, the sky, humanity. This is called "natural knowledge." The King of all creation proves His existence through the wonders of the universe. But there's more. God gives His children knowledge of His existence in His Word. The Bible reveals God and His kingdom (which includes us). God's Word is His precious gift to us so that we may know Him.

Humans are skeptics though, and so we question our Creator. We don't trust that the Bible is whole and perfect. We want to know more about God—we even want to *be* god. This lack of trust is the direct result of that brief conversation in the Garden of Eden between the evil one and our first parents. Since that moment, all people are born in a fallen world and in a sinful state. We doubt, we question, and we reject God and His gifts. Nevertheless, we are God's creation, so we want what He is and what He offers—peace, comfort, joy, hope, love, and life.

God wants this for us too. He doesn't want us to suffer, worry, fear, or hurt. He desires us to know Him and enjoy the blessings of the life He designed for us—the love of our family, the comfort of a hug, fellowship with other believers, forgiveness, mercy, and eternity with Him.

How do we get from the chaos caused by sin to the peace of God's presence? We live in a broken and messed-up world, and in turn, we live in brokenness. We are sinful. Satan puts up every barricade and stumbling block he can. There is nothing we can do to get to God's peace on our own.

Our Creator gives us the peace we can't reach on our own. He gives us His Son to resolve every sin and heal the broken world and our broken hearts. He gives us His Spirit to deliver faith, hope, and trust. We have His Word, living water, and His Holy Meal. These Means of Grace—physical things along with His Word—are so much a part of our daily lives and weekly routines that we might forget what they do for us.

God's Means of Grace are powerful and perfect. And they're real—God is present where they are. He is present in His Word. He is present in the gifts of Baptism. He is right there in the Holy Meal. And because we are His children—His beloved, redeemed, forgiven, saved children, made His own in Baptism and sustained in the Lord's Supper—God is with us where we are. It is because of these wondrous gifts that we have the peace of His presence.

He tells us all of this in the Bible. God reveals Himself in the recorded history of His people, in the psalms, the prophecies, the words of Jesus, and the words and writings of those He appointed to be His apostles. He also reveals Himself in the names He gives Himself.

Names in the Bible are significant because they describe a person's purpose, circumstances, or character. *Adam* comes from the Hebrew word for "ground." *Eve* means "mother of all the living." *Isaac* means "laughter." *Hannah* means "gracious." *Elizabeth* means "God's oath." And the names God uses for Himself teach us about Him. *Yahweh* (meaning the *LORD*, *Jehovah*), *Savior*, *Immanuel*, *Jehovah*, *Lord*, *Adonai*, and others. In fact, some translations identify as many as thirty names for God.

The original languages of the Bible—Hebrew and Greek—give different names for God that indicate different attributes and aspects of His character: a rock, a refuge, a dwelling place, a strong tower, love. We know Him better through His names when we understand what they mean. And while the English language doesn't have as many names for Him, we can study a reference to God in English and still appreciate the vivid imagery of the original languages.

Each chapter in this book focuses on one Hebrew name of God or a word or phrase that describes a characteristic or attribute of God or that describes something God does for us. As you consider each name, you will better understand how it describes unique aspects of God's character and how it communicates what He wants to relate to you.

As we begin, know you are God's precious child, called to Him by the water and Word of Baptism that made you His own. Nothing can separate you from your heavenly Father. No calamity, no sin, no other force can take you away from Him. Not even death—especially not death. When you spend time with God, His Holy Spirit fills you with His strength and power, and He provides you with a safe place.

Because you abide in the hope of the living God—in your Savior, Jesus—you can rest in the peace of His presence.

HOW TO USE THIS STUDY

Promised Rest: Finding Peace in God's Presence is an eight-week study for individuals and small groups. Each week is divided into five sessions—forty in total.

Each session includes personal reflection questions and discussion questions to deepen your understanding of the names and attributes of God we explore here. A small-group discussion guide is provided at the end of each chapter with answers to the discussion questions at the back of the book. And an ice-breaker activity for the first session is on page 226.

As you go through this study, give yourself grace. Be flexible. You will find what works best with your personal schedule and with your group's needs.

Bible Memory Verse

The introductory page for each week's study gives the name, characteristic, or action of God that is the focus for the week, as well as a Bible verse that either contains that name or illustrates the characteristic. Keep this verse in mind as you read the daily sessions, and commit it to memory.

Weekly Prayer

Throughout this study, I encourage you to create space for rest in the gift of prayer. Prayer draws you closer to the heavenly Father because it focuses you on your side of the conversation. God hears your prayer! His side of the conversation is your Bible.

The first session for each week offers a benediction and Scripture prayer. I encourage you to say both throughout the week, as often as you can.

A Scripture prayer is taken directly from the Bible and is one of the gifts of God's Word. He gives us the very words to say when we pray! The Holy Spirit works powerfully to direct our thinking toward God and His will for us.

The benediction, also called Aaron's Blessing and the priestly blessing, assures us of God's gifts and commitment to us:

> The LORD bless you and keep you;
> The LORD make His face to shine upon you and be gracious
> to you;
> The LORD lift up His countenance upon you and give you
> peace. (Numbers 6:24–26)

God gave these words to Moses, telling him to speak them to Aaron and his sons and to the children of Israel. We often hear this benediction at the close of the Divine Service. It brings to mind the three Persons of the Trinity and their blessings for us. God the Father, our Creator, blesses us with His goodness and provision. God the Son, the Redeemer and Light of the world, blesses us with favor and grace. God the Spirit, the Giver of life, blesses us by turning toward us and comforting us.

Saying this benediction reminds us of the very essence of who God is and what He does for us. Martin Luther said:

This blessing would ask the Lord God to lift up the light of His Word upon us and hold it above us so that it shines brighter and stronger in our heart than all the tribulation of the devil, death and sin, doubt, despair, terror, and all calamity can. . . . Then we will not only endure and at last overcome but also in the midst of this struggle and unrest have peace, praise and thank God, and not murmur or grow impatient with His divine will.[1]

God invites us to rest in the peace of His presence and to know that He is our Lord, who loves us beyond measure and who will work His will for us for our earthly and heavenly good.

DIRECTIONS FOR THE JOURNAL SPACE

Each session provides a space to journal about the lesson and a prompt to help you get started. At the journal prompt, reflect and remember what you learned from the day's session. Please know, some days you will have more time than others, but you can come back to the journal space throughout the day. It doesn't need to be done all at once.

Regarding the benefits and techniques of journaling, I have two questions for you:

- What do you cling to?
- When you have a challenge, face uncertainty, or something in your life is broken, where do you go for help?

Of course, the proper answer is that you cling to Christ, but I ask these questions because I struggle with this, and I suspect that other women do as well. Our culture teaches us to be self-sufficient and to be in control; we are led to believe that we don't need anyone. We are taught that we can overcome any circumstance, every challenge, and all uncertainty if only we try hard enough. But we know this simply isn't true.

The other day, I saw a meme of a man trying to mop up the ocean. The caption read, "This is what you look like when you are trying to control life."

Still, we try. Some people cling to their own ingenuity and determination. Some cling to tips and tricks and platitudes they find in social media. I am an emotional eater—I cling to food. If chocolate solved problems, mine would be gone. I also cling to my family and friends. I overthink and overtalk everything to the point of driving myself and everyone around me crazy. Can you relate?

God invites us to cling to Him. The word in Hebrew is *dabaq*, which means "to cling, to cleave, to be glued together." Look at this passage:

> For You have been my help, and in the shadow of Your wings
> I will sing for joy. My soul clings to You; Your right hand
> upholds me. (Psalm 63:7–8)

From this verse we learn:

- God is your help.
- As you cling to God, He holds you up and holds you close to Him.

By intentionally spending time in His presence, we can move from clinging to our own abilities to holding on to God. I've created a reflection exercise ("The Five *R*s," page 16) to this study that will help you remember to cling to God. As you practice reflection, you will find ways to use it throughout your day.

DISCUSSION AND REFLECTION QUESTIONS

Interspersed throughout each day's reading are two types of questions. Discussion questions are meant to be used in a group setting and are phrased so each participant will share openly and honestly what that week's study taught her about God's work in the world and in her life. Possible responses to the discussion questions are in the back of the book, beginning on page 218.

Reflection questions are personal. They are intended to help you go deeper into your faith life and to inspire you to explore how God's hand is on you in every aspect of your life. Reflection questions can help direct you as you journal, pray, and meditate on God's Word.

Visual Ministry

Finally, you will see scattered throughout this book illustrations reflecting the names and characteristics of God we study here. These illustrations are designed to appeal to your creative side and to help you visualize God's creative power and might in the big things and in the tiniest details. You may color these illustrations as you would any coloring book. You may use them in your meditation time to further that experience. Or you may leave them as is and simply enjoy the art. Visual ministry is meant to be as personal as your faith journal.

Conclusion

The peace of God's presence isn't far away; it's accessible right here and now for you as God's child. You don't need to earn your way into His presence, because peace is God's gift to you.

I encourage you as you go through this study to take the time for reflection and journaling. If you are not able to complete the activities in one sitting, come back to them or think about them throughout your day. The lasting benefit of these activities is to help you learn the names of God and see more clearly how your heavenly Father provides for you in each moment—giving you a deeper peace and a closer walk in His presence.

The Five *R*s of Reflection and Clinging Closer to God

REJOICE

- Write about what you are grateful or thankful for.
- Consider using this space as a gratitude or joy list.

RELEASE

- Which negative thoughts keep you awake at night and cause you to become stuck in the gloomy depths of pessimistic thinking?
- Do you feel shame over a past sin or decision that hangs over you like a cloud?
- What do you need to let go of that you cannot change?
- What hurts are you hanging on to?
- Write a prayer leaving all these things in the capable hands of God.

REFRAME

- What thoughts do you have about yourself, others, and God that need to change?
- Are there challenges or circumstances you need to see differently?
- What thoughts can you ask God to help you change?
- How do you talk about and see yourself? Think about how God sees you. What would He say to you?

REMEMBER

- What do you want to remember about God's name, characteristic, or action?
- What is something new you learned from today's session?
- What is one takeaway that you would like to remember?
- Spend time throughout the day remembering you are God's child.

REST

- What promise can you rest in today?
- What are some ways you can rest in the peace of God's presence?

Rejoice, Release, Reframe, Remember, and Rest

ELOHIM

Elohim: *Mighty, powerful*

Pronunciation: *el-o-heem'*

Elohim is mentioned 2,600 times in the Old Testament.

Bible Verse: *"Be still, and know that I am God." (Psalm 46:10a)*

DAY 1: ELOHIM CALLS YOU BY NAME

The universe is so vast, we cannot measure it in miles. We measure it in light-years. We know that light travels at 186,000 miles per second. One light-year equals about 6 trillion miles. Okay, let's geek out a bit here. How long would it take to travel one light-year? Let's imagine we had access to a spacecraft that traveled at 33,000 miles per hour. At that rate, it would take roughly six hours to go as far as light travels in one second. So, with current technology, we would need 21,600 years to cross the distance of one light-year. Earth is in the Milky Way galaxy, which is 100,000 light-years wide. So, if we hopped aboard our trusty spacecraft, our adventure would last more than 2 billion years.

The Andromeda galaxy is our nearest neighbor, at 2.537 million light-years (4 billion years by spacecraft) away. I cannot fathom it. When I stand and look at the magnitude of the night sky, it is incomprehensible and immeasurable. My mind wanders to the beginning, and I wonder what would it have been like to see the Creator unfold this masterpiece.

As we look at God's Word, the first place we see the name *Elohim* is at the very beginning, Genesis 1:1. In Hebrew, *Elohim* is plural. The triune God existed before He created the world; therefore, the nature of the Trinity is reflected in the name of God.

Genesis 1:1 refers to God as *Elohim*, which tells us that our Creator is mighty and powerful:

> In the beginning, God created the heavens and the earth.
> . . . And God said, "Let there be light," and there was light.
> (Genesis 1:1, 3)

What do you think about when you consider the strength and might Elohim used to create the universe? I cannot comprehend it.

By the word of the LORD the heavens were made, and by the
breath of His mouth all their host. He gathers the waters of
the sea as a heap; He puts the deeps in storehouses. Let all
the earth fear the LORD; let all the inhabitants of the world
stand in awe of Him! For He spoke, and it came to be; He
commanded, and it stood firm. (Psalm 33:6–9)

Elohim spoke the universe into existence. How did the light burst
forth? I envision a spectacular light show beyond any fireworks display I
have ever seen.

Imagine the wonder. Imagine the magnificence. The pure joy and delight as the persons of the Trinity watched the first glorious sunrise and
sunset. Consider that He had you and me in mind as He created the magnificent colors. All of creation points toward the glory of God, and you,
dear friend, are Elohim's masterpiece.

As we think about the name *Elohim*, it's important to remember God
as the three Persons of the Trinity. All things were created through the
Father, Son, and Holy Spirit. Elohim holds it all together. God the Son—
Jesus—was present at the moment of creation and before. He has always
existed and is our Creator.

He is the image of the invisible God, the firstborn of all
creation. For by Him all things were created, in heaven and
on earth, visible and invisible, whether thrones or domin-
ions or rulers or authorities—all things were created through
Him and for Him. And He is before all things, and in Him all
things hold together. (Colossians 1:15–17)

God is all-powerful and omnipotent beyond our imagination. Yet the
same God who created the universe—billions of galaxies and nanoparti-
cles of atoms—formed and molded us from the dust of the earth with His
hands. Our Creator spoke everything else into existence, but for us, He
used His hands. Elohim stitched you together in your mother's womb. He
isn't an abstract deity; He is right there with you.

As we consider all of creation, we understand God to be a fantastic artist.
Describe a marvelous sight you have seen in nature.

Why did Elohim do all this for you? Before the foundation of the world was laid, before the first grain of sand was created, the Lord God chose you to be His very own. Elohim knows you and loves you. He calls you by name. You can rest in His presence because that's where He wants you to be.

I will never forget the uncertainty I felt when my dad had his heart attack. I waited for news that the ambulance carrying him had arrived safely at the hospital. Even when I knew he was in the capable hands of the medical team, I worried. I prayed throughout the night: "God, may the doctors and nurses provide the best possible care for him. Please be with Dad and surround him with Your peace. Be near to Mom and give her comfort. In Jesus' name. Amen."

The next day, I paced in our living room while the boys played nearby with their toys. The phone rang, and my mom said, "I have someone who wants to talk to you." When I heard my dad's voice, I sank down on the couch. Relief spilled down my cheeks. We talked for a while, and I poured out my concerns. My dad gently reminded me, "Michelle, we can trust God."

Elohim held all things in His capable hands, and He held our family close to His heart. But how do we trust God when we receive news we do not want to hear? When our prayers are not answered in the way we had hoped? Elohim's promises are still true even when our hearts are broken. We can find comfort in knowing the Lord walks with us, even when it's a path we didn't choose. We can rest in the shelter of His presence, where He gives us His peace and the strength to face whatever comes next.

God makes these beautiful promises to each of us:

> But now thus says the LORD, He who created you, O Jacob,
> He who formed you, O Israel: "Fear not, for I have redeemed
> you; I have called you by name, you are Mine. When you
> pass through the waters, I will be with you; and through
> the rivers, they shall not overwhelm you; when you walk
> through fire you shall not be burned, and the flame shall not

consume you. For I am the LORD your God, the Holy One of Israel, your Savior." (Isaiah 43:1–3a)

Highlight or underline God's promises in this passage.

Discussion Question 1: What are God's promises to you in Isaiah 43:1–3? How can these promises comfort you in trying times?

Discussion Question 2: How might you approach each day differently, knowing Elohim calls you by name?

When was the last time you stood in wonder at God's creation? Go outside and listen to the melody of creation. What did you hear? Did you notice anything new?

Remember that your heavenly Father loves you. You are precious in His sight.

READ PSALM 46

This psalm teaches that you can dwell in the strength of Elohim. He provides a refuge for you in the peace of His presence. You can trust Him above all things. Even if it seems that your world is spinning out of control, you are secure in Him. Friend, you are God's precious child. He is faithful and will sustain and strengthen you to face all things.

The Hebrew word for God in verse 10 is *Elohim.* "Be still, and know that I am Elohim." "Be still" in Hebrew means "to loosen one's grip." Our natural reaction is to fix problems and control circumstances. We want to be in control. But when we put our trust in God to work all things for our good, we loosen our grip.

What are you holding onto that causes your soul to feel unsettled? Where do you need to loosen your grip? Ask Elohim to help you let go and place it in His hands. He cares about every detail. You are not alone.

SCRIPTURE PRAYER

How precious is Your steadfast love, O God! The children of mankind take refuge in the shadow of Your wings. (Psalm 36:7)

BENEDICTION

The LORD bless you and keep you;
The LORD make His face to shine upon you and be gracious
to you;
The LORD lift up His countenance upon you and give you
peace. (Numbers 6:24–26)

What are your favorite images from Psalm 46?

Refer to the exercise on page 16 to guide your journaling.

Day 2: When Life Is Uncertain

Some trust in chariots and some in horses, but we trust in the name of the LORD our God. (Psalm 20:7)

In the early morning hours, before the pink glow of dawn had chased away the midnight shadows, the phone rang. I was awake in an instant. My pulse raced and my mind spun with thoughts about my dad's condition. The phone call delivered the news that he had suffered another heart attack. The medical staff could not stop the attack and rushed him into surgery.

I wanted to be there, but a hospital waiting room is not a good place to keep two little boys occupied and quiet. My husband had just started a new job; it was impossible for him to take time off to be at home with them. Besides, my dad had said that the best place for me was to be at home with my boys. He assured me his doctors were excellent and he was in the hands of God. I knew he was right, but I was struggling between being a mom and being a daughter. My heart ached over not being at the hospital.

The surgery went as expected—everything appeared to be right on track. Dad faced some complications, but the doctors thought they were minor. However, throughout the day, the reports kept getting worse. My sister Sheila consulted a doctor friend who said we should be there. My twin sister, Jimella, and I had been in regular phone contact throughout the day, and we had already talked about heading north to be with our parents and other siblings. With the grim report, we made plans to travel. I had one major issue to figure out: *What do I do with the boys?*

It would be nearly impossible to find a babysitter to come every day before 4 a.m. after Troy went to work. How would I be able to leave them and still visit Dad? Just then, I got a phone call from my friend Melisa. "Michelle, let the boys stay with us while you are away. Go be with your dad." The relief and gratitude I felt at that moment moved me to tears.

Jimella arrived early the next morning and helped me get the boys to Melisa's house. Jacob and Matthew were excited to spend time with their friends; to them it was an extended slumber party.

As we began the seven-hour trip north, the unknown threatened to overwhelm us. Jimella said, "Let's not dwell on the what-ifs. We need to focus on our long drive." Tears pricked our eyes, but we sang our hearts out to songs from the eighties and lots of praise music. We shared favorite memories and reminiscences. There were moments when my mind wandered to dark places with unspeakable thoughts. I wanted to see my dad one more time. I longed to hold his hand, pray, encourage him, and tell him how much I love him. *Please, just one more time, God*, was the whisper of my heart.

When I am anxious and afraid, my thoughts spiral out of control. You too? When we stare death and hardship in the face, they can swallow us up, cloud our vision, and make us forget we are Elohim's children. Peace cannot be found in what we know about ourselves; the source of peace is God Himself.

> Behold, God is my helper; the Lord is the upholder of my
> life. (Psalm 54:4)

Who is the first person you go to when you need help? What does God invite us to do?

We kept in contact with our mom by cell phone on the long trip north. Dad was critical, but remained stable. When we were finally there, Jimella and I found the ICU waiting room where our mom and siblings were. We embraced one another with words inexpressible. The five of us were held together by a lifetime of love and memories. Even though the air hung heavy with uncertainty, hope remained. Elohim was with us.

My mom grabbed Jimella and me by the hand. "I'm so glad you're here. Sheila, David, and I just saw Dad. The doctors allow visitors for only five minutes every hour so he can rest."

"Can't we go in now to see him?" Surely the doctors would recognize that Jimella and I had just arrived and were longing to see him.

Mom continued, "They have him in a medically induced coma, and the best thing you can do for your dad is to wait. I know it's hard. When we do see him, we have to keep emotion and fear out of our voices, because it's important for him to remain calm." I took in the information, thankful for time to prepare myself to visit him in that state.

Finally, it was time for me to see Dad for the first time since his heart attack and surgery. The first time since my last visit eight months ago. I had prayed all day for this moment, asking God to help me be strong for Dad, for Mom, and for my siblings. Jesus walked with me across the threshold of my dad's ICU room. I looked around the room at the massive amount of equipment keeping my dad alive. His face was swollen from the fluids they were pumping through him to keep his body working. Fear swelled over the barriers I tried to raise in my mind. I wanted to run away as fast as I could, because the man lying there was not the healthy and robust father I knew. This man was fragile, and his life seemed finite; I was not ready to imagine my life without him. The presence of Elohim gave me a refuge as I looked at my dad. And I didn't run, because I remembered the Lord's strength was what held us together.

God gave me the presence of mind to stay calm, and He provided the right words to say. I leaned in close and whispered a phrase adapted from Psalm 62 into my beloved father's ear. "My soul finds rest in God alone." I took comfort knowing those words were just as much a gift for me as they were for him.

Five minutes went by too fast. As I left the room, my tears came. I could hear my dad's voice in my head: "You need to help take care of your mom." As hard as it was on all of us kids, I knew Mom struggled most. I couldn't imagine what it was like for her to watch her husband, best friend, and the love of her life lying in a hospital bed.

Waiting defines life in the ICU. Waiting for test results, doctor visits, to see a loved one, to breathe normally again. The sights and sounds of the ICU filled me with horror and dread. I confess that at times I forgot about

God's sovereignty. But we still had God's overwhelming love and power. He is our fortress.

Soak in the words of Psalm 27:1: "The LORD is my light and my salvation; whom shall I fear? The LORD is the stronghold of my life; of whom shall I be afraid?"

Notice how this passage is written in the present tense; that means it's happening now. The Lord is your light. He is your salvation. The Lord is your stronghold, your place of refuge. What a comfort to know Elohim provides a place of refuge for you all the days of your life.

Discussion Question 3: What causes you to fear or be afraid? Bring your fear before the Lord in prayer.

> When evildoers assail me to eat up my flesh, my adversaries and foes, it is they who stumble and fall. Though an army encamp against me, my heart shall not fear; though war arise against me, yet I will be confident. One thing have I asked of the LORD, that will I seek after: that I may dwell in the house of the LORD all the days of my life, to gaze upon the beauty of the LORD and to inquire in His temple. (Psalm 27:2–4)

The house of the Lord has always been a place to receive the gifts of grace from God. Those gifts strengthen us while we wait.

> For He will hide me in His shelter in the day of trouble; He will conceal me under the cover of His tent; He will lift me high upon a rock. (Psalm 27:5)

Trouble will come and continue in this world, but we are safe within the shelter of Elohim.

Discussion Question 4: How does knowing that Elohim shelters you through trouble change how you look at adversity?

> Hide not Your face from me. Turn not Your servant away in anger, O You who have been my help. Cast me not off; forsake me not, O God of my salvation! (Psalm 27:9)

In this verse, the name of God is Elohim. We are reminded once again that God is our help; He will never abandon or forsake us. Trouble will come because the world is sinful and broken, but Elohim will not turn away from us. He is with us through all things.

> I believe that I shall look upon the goodness of the LORD in the land of the living! Wait for the LORD; be strong, and let your heart take courage; wait for the LORD! (Psalm 27:13–14)

Some translations say the Lord will "strengthen" your heart. How do you need God to strengthen your heart today?

Refer to the exercise on page 16 to guide your journaling.

DAY 3: THE PRESENCE OF ELOHIM

My presence will go with you, and I will give you rest.
(Exodus 33:14)

My dad was in the ICU for twelve days. Each time we visited him, we sang for him quietly, and his blood pressure always improved. He was responding to our voices while still in a coma. The nurses encouraged us to keep singing—Dad was listening.

One day, while we sang "Amazing Grace," the chaplain stopped at the door of my dad's room and joined in our singing. Afterward, he said, "So you're the angels in the ICU. The patients around here wait for the singing to start each hour." We were surprised, because we tried to sing as quietly as possible. He said, "Your voices do carry, and I am thankful because it brings peace and comfort to the patients. You are not disturbing anyone."

Even though I walk through the valley of the shadow of
death, I will fear no evil, for You are with me; Your rod and
Your staff, they comfort me. (Psalm 23:4)

Looking back, I see how our faith in God sustained us. People all over the world prayed for our dad. Our brothers and sisters in Christ walked with us and held us up with their love and kindness. And God heard our prayers!

Eventually, my dad improved enough to move out of the ICU and into rehabilitative care to receive physical therapy that helped build up his strength. He was hospitalized for five weeks. Thirteen years later, he is still with us.

One of my dad's favorite Bible passages is Isaiah 40:28–31:

Have you not known? Have you not heard? The LORD is the
everlasting God, the Creator of the ends of the earth. He does

not faint or grow weary; His understanding is unsearchable. He gives power to the faint, and to him who has no might He increases strength. Even youths shall faint and be weary, and young men shall fall exhausted; but they who wait for the LORD shall renew their strength; they shall mount up with wings like eagles; they shall run and not be weary; they shall walk and not faint.

Eagles flap their wings only a few minutes per hour, because flapping takes an extreme amount of energy. The rest of the time, they soar on air currents, which allows them to conserve energy. After being in the ICU for so long, my dad had to rebuild his strength to do even normal, everyday activities we take for granted. Getting out of bed, walking, at first even standing all took an extreme amount of energy as he was recovering. However, even though Dad was physically weak, God gave him the strength of will to put one foot in front of the other. What's more, Dad's faith in God to be with him, and in God's will for his life, never wavered.

God does the same for us. We never face trials and challenges on our own strength; rather, we rely on God's mercy and wait for God's will to be done. Elohim gives us His power.

Discussion Question 5: Reflect and think about a time when you were weary and God strengthened you. How did He increase your strength?

My dad doesn't remember much from his time in the ICU, but he does have one vivid memory. He remembers waking up and seeing the machines around him performing tasks that his body couldn't do on its own. As his awareness of the circumstances grew, my dad found comfort in remembering that God is always with him. He didn't know the answers, but God gave him the peace of His presence.

READ PSALM 18:1—6

In this passage we see the following:

- David is praising God for delivering him from King Saul.

- This psalm is similar to 2 Samuel 22. Both passages recount or remember what God has done for David.
- David found his security in Elohim.

Discussion Question 6: What images come to your mind as you think about Elohim as your fortress? A fortress provides exceptional security. Some translations call it a stronghold.

How has God been your fortress? Maybe you didn't realize it in the moment, but you can see how Elohim protected you as you look back.

If you were to write a psalm about what God has done for you, what would you include? What would you like your children and grandchildren to know about what God has done for you in your life? This reflection could take a while; I invite you to take your time with it. If you have the time, look at each decade of your life and write about the events you can remember. Whether you knew it or not at the time, Elohim was with you every minute.

Some of your memories might be painful and stir up grief; please know I am praying for you. Elohim is right here with you, holding you as you remember. Pour out your heart before Him; you can trust Him.

Reflect on what God has done in your life. Remembering how God has helped us in the past and how He promises to help us throughout our earthly lives strengthens our faith and allows us to face our daily challenges.

Refer to the exercise on page 16 to guide your journaling.

Day 4: Pour Out Your Heart

In Genesis 1–2, we glimpse the perfection of the Garden of Eden and see the beauty Elohim created. As we linger in those chapters, we see the world as God intended. The Garden is paradise, and the people living there are perfect images of God. There was no decay, no destruction, no death. The beginning of God's Word shows us what we can expect in heaven with Him. I find myself wanting to linger there, in God's paradise, because I know everything is going to change in Genesis 3. The serpent slithers in and sows seeds of doubt. Sin enters the picture because Eve and Adam did not trust God.

We live in a sinful world. We cannot separate our lives from sin. A stain has seeped into our lives, and we weep and wail in the wreckage of the original relationship God designed to have with us.

Nearly losing my dad forced me to understand that someday I will face the deaths of those I dearly love. And those I dearly love will face my death.

Death isn't fair, and it isn't part of God's plan. Death causes deep sorrow and sometimes hardship. We feel powerless when we realize we cannot bargain with death or control it. Our self-reliance crumbles because we know human effort can never make it go away.

Helpless, we cry out to God as the devil whispers words of doubt and despair into our minds. Such words have been echoing since that moment in the garden. Oh, friends, Satan wants to stir confusion and keep our focus off the promises of God. But God's Word is louder than the evil one's whisper. In Genesis 3:15, Elohim vows to send a Savior to conquer sin, death, and the devil. And He does. Jesus is that Savior, the fulfillment of the promise.

However, we are descendants of Eve and Adam. If we are left to our own devices, sin would leave us abandoned on a path of destruction. Mercifully, Jesus steps into our brokenness and holds us close. He guides us safely back into communion with the Father. Sin does not win; even when we cannot see through the pain, Jesus has the final say.

Death comes, but it does not write the ending of our stories. Our Savior, the author and perfecter of our faith, rewrote death's story by His death on the cross. Eternal life belongs to God's children.

> For the wages of sin is death, but the free gift of God is eternal life in Christ Jesus our Lord. (Romans 6:23)

Life often throws us curveballs, leaving us unprepared to face what comes next. But Elohim wants us to trust Him.

How does it make a difference knowing Elohim provides a refuge for us when we face trials?

We can find some answers in Psalm 57. David wrote this psalm while he was hiding from King Saul in a cave.

> Be merciful to me, O God, be merciful to me, for in You my soul takes refuge; in the shadow of Your wings I will take refuge, till the storms of destruction pass by. (Psalm 57:1)

No matter how big or small our challenges, God invites us to pour out our hearts before Him, and David shows us how in this beautiful psalm.

God invites you to take refuge in Him. What storms are you facing in your life?

He is with you in everything you are facing, and He will never leave you.

> I cry out to God Most High, to God who fulfills His purpose for me. He will send from heaven and save me; He will put to shame him who tramples on me. God will send out His steadfast love and His faithfulness! (Psalm 57:2–3)

Pour your heart out before Him. Look at the gifts Elohim sends you! Use an online dictionary to find the definition of these words, or write what they mean to you:

- Steadfastness: _____

- Faithfulness: _____

Discussion Question 7: How does knowing that Elohim sends you His steadfastness and faithfulness change how you face difficult circumstances?

> My soul is in the midst of lions; I lie down amid fiery
> beasts—the children of man, whose teeth are spears and
> arrows, whose tongues are sharp swords. (Psalm 57:4)

What lions do you face right now?

> Be exalted, O God, above the heavens! Let Your glory be over
> all the earth! (Psalm 57:5)

Verses five and eleven in the psalm are precisely the same. In them, David praises God even before God delivers him. David praises God while he is concealed in the caves.

Discussion Question 8: How can you glorify God right now? If you cannot think of what to say, is there a song you can sing or listen to?

> They set a net for my steps; my soul was bowed down. They
> dug a pit in my way, but they have fallen into it themselves.
> My heart is steadfast, O God, my heart is steadfast! I will sing
> and make melody! (Psalm 57:6–7)

The gifts God gave to David have now strengthened His heart with steadfastness.

How do you need God to strengthen your heart today?

> Awake, my glory! Awake, O harp and lyre! I will awake the
> dawn! I will give thanks to You, O Lord, among the peoples; I
> will sing praises to You among the nations. For Your steadfast
> love is great to the heavens, Your faithfulness to the clouds.
> Be exalted, O God, above the heavens! Let Your glory be over
> all the earth! (Psalm 57:8–11)

How can you see God's glory today? Perhaps you can spend some time outside and rest in the glory of His creation.

Refer to the exercise on page 16 to guide your journaling.

Day 5: Red Sea Moments

Have you noticed how you can read a portion of Scripture many times, and each time, Elohim teaches you something new about who He is and how His promises are true and applicable for your life? God's Word continuously transforms us and changes how we view life. It is more powerful than we can possibly imagine. His Word created the universe out of nothing, created the microscopic building blocks of human life, commanded the earth to obey Him—and brought life out of death.

Have you ever had a Red Sea moment—the feeling of being stuck in an impossible situation?

Sometimes we see only the options that fill our hearts with terror. The Israelites thought they were trapped between two horrific deaths: slaughter at the hands of Pharaoh's ferocious army, or drowning in the insurmountable Red Sea.

Let's imagine ourselves in the story. Can you hear the roar of the sea? Panic fills your thoughts as you gaze at the water and waves. Before you even look over your shoulder, you feel the ground shake from the six hundred chariots of the Egyptian army. You turn and see the horsemen—fifty thousand of them!—arrayed for battle. In the distance, you hear the thunder of eighty thousand soldiers' feet.

As a slave in Egypt, you knew firsthand the cruelty of Pharaoh and his army. Alarm and disbelief rise within you. You question Elohim, and anger stirs your thoughts against Moses. Why did he lead us out here to our death?

Still, you follow Moses. What else can you do? The spray from the Red Sea splashes against your feet. The salt water mixes with the desert dust and your tears of dread, and your eyes sting from the combination. You wipe your eyes to see, but you're tempted to cover your face to stop the terror that is rising from within you.

Then, above all the noise, drowning out even your own panic, is the voice of Moses:

> And Moses said to the people, "Fear not, stand firm, and see the salvation of the LORD, which He will work for you today. For the Egyptians whom you see today, you shall never see again. The LORD will fight for you, and you have only to be silent." (Exodus 14:13–14)

Elohim directs Moses to raise his staff. And when he does, the deep water stirs and the sea parts. God holds back the water. The ground is dry enough for you and the hundreds of thousands with you to cross safely to the other side.

The angel of God moves behind you as a pillar of cloud, separating you from the Egyptians. Your mighty Elohim stands guard, providing protection against Pharaoh's army in a way you never could have imagined.

Once you and the rest of the Israelites cross, the pillar of cloud moves in front of you. The Egyptian army races onto the path through the sea, but God releases the waters. The torrent rushes back together, obliterating Pharaoh's army.

Fear caused the Israelites to forget they were God's chosen people, and it makes us forget we are God's children. But Elohim has command of all. He planned for the Israelites to be delivered across the Red Sea in a way that defies our rational thought, and He rescues us in radical ways too.

Some translations, instead of saying, "Be silent," say, "Be still." The Israelites had to trust Elohim to deliver them from their trouble. There was nothing they could have done to solve the dilemma on their own. Elohim stepped in and caused the water to part so the Israelites could walk across on dry land.

Up until this point, God had gone before them in the pillar of cloud. At the crossing, He moved behind them to block the Egyptians from seeing what was going on. Elohim took care of every detail. God stepped in with a solution they couldn't have imagined. When we face a problem or a challenge, we think of it only from our human perspective. We place God within our finite view and forget He is infinite. Sometimes we even tell God how He might solve our difficulties. Repeatedly, He steps in and shows us a far better way.

Discussion Question 9: Have you ever faced a situation in which the only thing you could do was to be still and remember that God was God? What was it?

Discussion Question 10: How might knowing God as Elohim help you face an impossible situation in the future?

God tells us over and over again in Scripture to remember what He has done. Memories can stir up powerful emotions, but memory is subjective. When you focus on who God is and what He has already done for you, it will help you remember how God will help you in the future.

At the beginning of the lesson, I asked if you had ever had a Red Sea moment. You and I both have: the moment sin entered the world. Humanity, in our fallen state, faced an impossible situation—eternal separation from God, eternal damnation in hell. Stuck in our sin, we could not get out. Only God is equipped to save. He sent His Son, Jesus, to rescue us. Through the water of Holy Baptism with God's Word, we are brought into the family of God. Just as Elohim led the children of Israel through the water of the Red Sea, He leads us through the water of Baptism and saves us.

What do you know or remember about your Baptism?

What are some ways you can meditate on God as Elohim? Here are a few ideas:

- Find or take a picture of a favorite place.
- Write a story or paint a picture to recall a time Elohim gave you strength.
- Create a special area outside where you can sit or spend time in Elohim's presence.

Refer to the exercise on page 16 to guide your journaling.

Week 1 Group Study Questions

Elohim

Elohim: *Mighty, powerful*

Pronunciation: *el-o-heem'*

Elohim is mentioned 2,600 times in the Old Testament.

Bible Verse: *"Be still, and know that I am God."* (Psalm 46:10a)

REFLECTIONS

- What story stood out to you the most from this week's sessions? Why?
- What did you learn about God as Elohim?

DISCUSSION QUESTIONS (FROM THE DAILY SESSIONS)

1. What are God's promises to you in Isaiah 43:1–3? How can these promises comfort you in trying times?

2. How might you approach each day differently, knowing Elohim calls you by name?

3. What causes you to fear or be afraid? Bring your fear before the Lord in prayer.

4. How does knowing that Elohim shelters you through trouble change how you look at adversity?

5. Reflect and think about a time when you were weary and God strengthened you. How did He increase your strength?

6. What images come to your mind as you think about Elohim as your fortress? A fortress provides exceptional security. Some translations call it a stronghold.

7. How does knowing that Elohim sends you His steadfastness and faithfulness change how you face difficult circumstances?

8. How can you glorify God right now? If you cannot think of what to say, is there a song you can sing or listen to?

9. Have you ever faced a situation in which the only thing you could do was to be still and remember that God was God? What was it?

10. How might knowing God as Elohim help you face an impossible situation in the future?

To close our first week, let's spend time with the benediction from Numbers 6:24–26:

> The LORD bless you and keep you;
> The LORD make His face to shine upon you and be gracious
> to you;
> The LORD lift up His countenance upon you and give you
> peace.

Be in the presence of the One (Elohim) who breathed into you the breath of life. He has called you by name. He holds you in His capable hands. May you rest in His promises, this week and always.

ABBA

Abba: *The closest word for* Abba *in the English language is "Papa" or "Daddy."*

Pronunciation: *ab-bah'*

Abba *is used only three times in Scripture, but each instance points us to God as our Father. We have been adopted into God's family through Jesus.*

Bible Verse: *"See what kind of love the Father has given to us, that we should be called children of God; and so we are. The reason why the world does not know us is that it did not know Him." (1 John 3:1)*

Day 1: You Are Abba's Beloved Child

Aquanet swirled through the bathroom like mosquito fogger mist, and the scent of Jean Naté lingered in the air. I peered into the mirror after struggling with my hair for forty minutes; it looked acceptable, but I couldn't spend any more time on it. If I didn't get out the door in the next five minutes, I'd be late catching the church bus for the annual youth group hayride.

Racing through the house, I grabbed my winter coat and gloves and was finally ready to leave. I leaned down to give my dad a quick kiss on my way out the door. He glanced up and said, "You need to wear a hat; it's going to be cold."

How many times would my dad say those exact words to me? Annoyance snarled through the air. "No way."

He continued, and my impatience brewed: "You lose 80 percent of your body heat from an uncovered head. I don't want you getting sick."

I had asthma, and cold air triggered it. Frustration and fear of being late caused the squabble to turn into a one-sided shouting match. Dad only slightly raised his voice; I supplied most of the volume. How could he suggest wearing a hat, given how long it took me to fix my hair? But he wouldn't budge. In desperation and defiance, I looked right at him and said, "If I get cold, I'll just put up the hood of my coat." We both knew that was a lie.

I stomped my way down the stairs, slamming the door behind me and running to catch up with my twin sister, Jimella, who had already left the house.

By the time I reached the bus, my haughtiness cooled by the biting wind, I was already feeling guilty about my awful behavior. I had never left the house being angry at my parents. Usually, after an argument, I would simmer for a while, then remember how much they loved me and apologize. My dad worked long, back-breaking hours at our local paper mill, and he never complained. Love for his family fueled his determination to provide for us by working hard and putting up with guff from an impatient teenage girl.

I had always been close with my dad, so the discord I caused bothered me. The bus pulled away, and since cell phones were a few decades from being in everyone's pockets, I couldn't call. There was no opportunity to make it right.

I got off the bus at the parking lot where the tractor and hay wagons waited. Crisp, cool air tingled against my cheeks; leaves crackled and crunched beneath my feet; if I'd had a hat, I would have put it on. My thoughts lingered for a few moments over the angry words I had thrown at my dad an hour before.

Why did I say things I didn't mean?

Remorse stirred in my soul, and I vowed to apologize to my dad as soon as I got home. Then, letting go of what I could not repair at the moment, delight bubbled to the surface as I joined the fun happening around me. The October night filled with laughter as I scrambled onto the second wagon with my friends. The tractor lurched forward with enough power to pull both wagons over the winding gravel road.

My heart danced with joyfulness as the singing began. The night held the promise of merriment and adventure. Jimella and I sang with the rest of the youth group, giggling when one wagon's song was slightly ahead of the other.

Then the happy singing turned to terror-filled screams as the tractor picked up speed down a hill. The back wagon fishtailed, flinging hay bales and teenagers against the sides. Fear gripped my heart, and I lunged forward to grab hold of my sister to keep her from flying off the wagon. Instead, I was the one who fell. I felt myself slipping over the front of the wagon and hurtling toward the ground.

When I came to, I was initially aware only of the cold ground and sharp gravel. I stared into the black velvet sky and didn't know where I was. "Why am I lying on the ground?"

Jimella cried out, "Oh no, she has amnesia!"

My memories surged and became untangled. I had been thrown from the wagon! I was cold, and my head throbbed. (I learned later that I had been knocked out by the hitch.) When I tried to move, someone cautioned me to lie still, warning of broken bones. One of the chaperones had run to a nearby farmhouse and called 911—the ambulance was on the way. Words intending to comfort me instead left me to wonder if something was seriously wrong.

Jimella knelt on the cold ground and held my hand. All we could do was wait. Finally, the sirens screeched in and the group stepped back and grew silent as EMTs raced toward me with a stretcher.

My parents met us at the hospital, and I caught a glimpse of their worried faces as I was whisked through the emergency room doors. Then the tears came as I remembered the angry words I had hurled at my dad. The doctors wheeled me past him, and an apology tumbled out of my mouth. Dad told me it was okay. "I love you, Michelle. I forgive you."

The doctors poked and prodded, and after several X-rays, they decided I needed to stay in the hospital for further testing. My ankle was sprained and strained and had a hairline fracture. One of my ribs had a hairline crack. I had a concussion. And they were concerned about internal bleeding and damage to my kidneys.

Mom went home with my three siblings, and Dad stayed with me. I knew he was tired; he had worked a lot of sixteen-hour days that week, but he never mentioned being weary. His gentle presence reminded me that he loved me. I drifted in and out of sleep, and every time I woke, Dad was holding my hand securely in his, an assurance that I could rely on him.

After a long, tiring night, I looked at my dad and said, "Thank you for sitting with me all night holding my hand." He said, "I love you. And I am glad I could be here for you."

When the ambulance had arrived at the scene, the chaperones told the

EMTs they thought I had been run over by the hay wagon. After I fell, the passengers felt the wagon jolt and shudder as if rolling over something in the road. Yet when they looked, there was nothing in the road. No bale of straw or tree branch or other obstruction. There was nothing else that could have explained why they all felt the same sensation. Still, the injuries I sustained were not consistent with someone who had been run over. There was no explanation, but in my mind, there was only one possibility—God had protected me from those wagon wheels.

Our heavenly Father held me in His capable hands during that hayride, through the long night, and beyond. The testing showed I had a bruised kidney. Because of internal bleeding, I stayed in the hospital for nine days, and I missed a month of school while I recuperated.

Our earthly fathers have an impact on how we view God as our heavenly Father. If your father is kind and loving, you think of that example when contemplating God as Father. Conversely, if your father was abusive or was absent, then your image of a father includes heartache and pain. You may wince when you hear God called *father*.

God's Word paints a picture of Abba, our dear Father in heaven. God is tender and filled with compassion. God's love for you is unconditional. His Holy Word reminds you not only of who He is but also who you are in Him. God has chosen you and loves you beyond measure.

> Blessed be the God and Father of our Lord Jesus Christ, who
> has blessed us in Christ with every spiritual blessing in the
> heavenly places, even as He chose us in Him before the foun-
> dation of the world, that we should be holy and blameless
> before Him. (Ephesians 1:3–4)

You have received every spiritual blessing, in Christ, through the waters of Holy Baptism, and God has adopted you and called you to be His precious child.

How does it make you feel to know that you are Abba's beloved child and are precious to Him?

Discussion Question 11: What is or was your relationship with your earthly father? How has it affected how you see God as your Father?

Discussion Question 12: What are some ways you can remember that God is your Abba Father daily? Here are a couple ideas to add to your own:

- Make the sign of the cross when you wake up and when you go to bed to remember your Baptism and that you have been marked with the cross of Christ forever.
- Pray the Lord's Prayer and reflect on this explanation from the Small Catechism.

  ### The Introduction
  ### Our Father who art in heaven.

  What does this mean?
  With these words God tenderly invites us to believe that He is our true Father and that we are His true children, so that with all boldness and confidence we may ask Him as dear children ask their dear father.[2]

SCRIPTURE PRAYER

Now Jesus was praying in a certain place, and when He finished, one of His disciples said to Him, "Lord, teach us to pray, as John taught his disciples." And He said to them, "When you pray, say: 'Father, hallowed be Your name. Your kingdom come. Give us each day our daily bread, and forgive us our sins, for we ourselves forgive everyone who is indebted to us. And lead us not into temptation.'" (Luke 11:1–4)

BENEDICTION

The LORD bless you and keep you;
The LORD make His face to shine upon you and be gracious to you;
The LORD lift up His countenance upon you and give you peace. (Numbers 6:24–26)

Describe how you felt the first time you realized what it meant to be God's beloved child.

Day 2: Abba's Gift of Grace

Today, let's consider the story of the prodigal son, as told in Luke 15:11–32. Notice especially how the father responds to both of his sons. This is Jesus revealing to us our Abba Father and the ways He shows His love to us.

When we read this passage through the lens of our twenty-first-century experiences, it's easy to miss some critical points of understanding of first-century Jewish culture.

When the younger son asked for his share of the inheritance, in essence, he was saying, "I wish you were dead." Nevertheless, the father graciously gave the son his inheritance. All their assets would have been in the farm, so a portion of the family's land and animals would need to be sold to provide the son with his share. Selling a part of the farm would mean fewer crops, a reduced food supply, and diminished ability to make money from the harvest. The father gave the older son his share of the inheritance too. So the father gave everything to his children while he was still living.

The younger son went off and spent all his money on extravagant living. It is often said he spent it on immoral living, but we only hear that from his angry and judgmental older brother. After squandering his inheritance, the son took a job feeding pigs, which made him unclean according to Jewish law.

The son was hungry and desperate for food. He remembered that his father's servants were well cared for and never went hungry. He decided to go home and ask his father for a job, because he believed he was no longer worthy of being called his father's son. The father must have been watching and waiting for the son to come home, because he saw him from a far-off distance. The father had compassion toward the son and raced to meet him. The father would have had to gather up his robes to run to his son. Middle Eastern men did not run, and they certainly would not have bared their legs; that would have brought humiliation to the family. But in Jesus' parable, it didn't matter to the father how he looked. The father was happy to see his son and anxious to get to him before the villagers did.

If a first-century Jewish child lost his family inheritance amongst the Gentiles or married outside the faith, the community would perform a cutting-off ceremony to prevent the person from returning home. They would break a pot in front of the errant child and cry out, "You are cut off from your people." This ceremony is called the *Kezazah*, and once it was performed, the community would have nothing to do with the cast-out person.

The father ran to embrace his son, kissed him, and showed the community he accepted his son and welcomed him home. The son was fully aware of the *Kezazah* and the significance of his father's act of love. The words spilled forth from the son's mouth: "I am no longer worthy of being called your son; I have sinned against heaven and you" (see verse 21). At that moment, the younger son placed his broken, messed-up life in his father's hands.

We watch this story unfold from our viewpoint. Yes, the son now seems sorry, but look at the mess. We anticipate a scene in which the father reads off the list of every offense the son has committed. Instead, we see grace and mercy wrapped in the perfect love the father has for his son. Before the son could even begin to confess his sins, the father plans a party to welcome his son back. He didn't condemn his son. He didn't tell him he was disappointed in his behavior or that he had brought shame to the family name. He showed love, compassion, mercy, and grace.

The father restored his son's position in the family in front of all the people in the village. The son knew he could not fix what had been done, but he brought the broken pieces of his life before the father anyway. Grace flowed and poured out over the son from the father. The father collected the shattered fragments and completely restored his son's life.

How many times do we try to hide from God when we have sinned?

We know we have disappointed Him by our shameful behaviors and by putting our selfish desires ahead of what He asks of us. We are afraid to come before the Father, the One who created us in His image, because we have created God in our own image. This places human limitations upon the heavenly Father and expects His response to be like our own. However, the father of the prodigal shows us that God's way is always filled with unending grace and love.

When you have time, read all of Luke 15. This chapter contains the three parables of the lost, which Jesus told in response to the Pharisees and scribes grumbling about Jesus eating with sinners. These are the main points Jesus makes in Luke 15:

- God cares for and loves the lost.
- We were lost in our sins until Jesus claimed us through the waters of Holy Baptism.
- God will seek us relentlessly until we return to Him.

God continuously calls His people back into fellowship with Him. He loves us however we are and wherever we are. These stories are the opposite of how we think and view life when it comes to acceptance and forgiveness.

Discussion Question 13: Do you try to hide your sin from God? Why or why not?

READ ISAIAH 55:6—9

Read this passage slowly and savor it. Take some time to highlight and underline. I used to skim through the first part to get to my favorite verses, but I have realized that by doing so, I missed some important truths.

- It's hard for us to understand how much our Abba Father loves us, because we don't think the same way He does.
- Maybe you are like me and you try to "pretty up" your sins before God. You want to justify or explain them away and tell God why you did what you did.
- God wants us to come to Him and confess our sins, and when we do, He removes them from us. So many times, we stay stuck in our sin because we feel such shame and sorrow over them, and that's understandable.

- The devil would love for the *Kezazah* (cutting off) ceremony to be performed on you, to convince you that God wants to break away from you and that you should be separated forever from your Abba Father because of your sin.
- God the Father runs to you in the waters of Holy Baptism and claims you as His own. He runs to you in His Word and pours out His peace and promises to you. He welcomes you into the family and lavishes you with the gifts of grace. He offers Himself to you in the Holy Feast, where He forgives your sins and strengthens you for the days ahead.

Discussion Question 14: What would the Father say to you right now if you confessed your sins to Him and repented of them? How would He look at you?

Here's the truth: God is God. His thoughts are so much higher than ours. We can't possibly comprehend the mind of God because of our human limitations. Jesus' parable of the prodigal son shows that God's love for you is not bound by your ability to comprehend or even begin to understand it. It is beyond measure.

Take some time to talk to God and confess your sins to Him. Place your sins into the nail-scarred capable hands of Jesus, and leave them there. You don't need to take your sins back; He has removed them from you.

Day 3: Your Sin Is Removed

In the parable of the prodigal son, we might think of the older son as the obedient, good son, because he appears to follow all the rules. But let's look at the parable through the lens of first-century Jewish customs.

As the older brother came in from the fields, he heard lively music and realized a party was going on. He stopped a young boy and asked him what was happening. The boy told him, "Your younger brother has returned, and your father has restored his relationship with him. He is no longer lost" (see Luke 15:26–27). Now, one would think that the older brother would feel relief at this fantastic news, but instead he stood outside sulking and pouting in a cloud of self-pity.

According to Jewish custom, sons would stand by their father's side to receive guests; even if they could not stay for the party, they would give honor by greeting people as they arrived. The older son would know that it was an insult not to welcome the guests. But he rejected his responsibilities as the son of the host; he refused to come to the party. The older son's action was an intentional insult to his father; it may even have been a worse insult than the younger son's, because it was a public rejection.

All the guests were aware of what was going on. Everyone waited to see what the father would do. He had every right to punish this son—but that was not what he did. Instead, we see a loving father trying to reason with his son and restore what had been broken.

The older son didn't want to listen. He talked about all the things he had done right. He cared deeply about keeping the law and about getting his just share of the inheritance. But he didn't care about restoring the relationship with his brother or about his father's love for them both. The father's heart was again broken, but he offered grace and compassion.

Discussion Question 15: To which of the sons in the parable of the prodigal son do you relate the most? Why?

I relate to both sons. I am both the good son, doing what is expected of me, and the bad son, doing what I want to do. In this parable, Jesus wants us to recognize ourselves in both sons and to note that the father is the one who reaches out to restore both relationships.

What does that tell us? Our heavenly Father is always the one who reaches out to us. He is the one who makes restoration possible. This parable is about what God does for us even though we sin against Him, not what we do for Him in our faith.

Sometimes we get stuck thinking we can earn God's love or that we need to earn His favor. Our human minds try to put God within our humanness. It doesn't work.

> If You, O LORD, should mark iniquities, O Lord, who could
> stand? (Psalm 130:3)

God does not keep a record of our wrongs. He removes our sins from us and remembers them no more.

Abba's love for you is always based upon who He is. His heart for you is filled with loving kindness.

God the Father loves you. His love and compassion toward you have no limits. His love defies our human understanding. When you feel remorse over your actions that resemble those committed by either of the brothers in the parable, be assured that God wants you to return to Him. And because Jesus paid the price, you can come before the Father and confess your sins. He is watching and waiting for you to come to Him. He wants to hear you confess and repent of your sins. He races to you and lavishes His love upon you. He gives you everything you need.

Find comfort in the words of Psalm 103:12–13. Highlight and underline these verses in your Bible. Just as it is impossible for the east and the west ever to meet, your sins will not come back to you. When Jesus said, "It is finished," on the cross, He said it for you. The debt you owed has been paid in full.

You are forgiven!

But God, being rich in mercy, because of the great love with which He loved us, even when we were dead in our trespasses, made us alive together with Christ—by grace you have been saved—and raised us up with Him and seated us with Him in the heavenly places in Christ Jesus, so that in the coming ages He might show the immeasurable riches of His grace in kindness toward us in Christ Jesus. For by grace you have been saved through faith. And this is not your own doing; it is the gift of God, not a result of works, so that no one may boast. For we are His workmanship, created in Christ Jesus for good works, which God prepared beforehand, that we should walk in them. (Ephesians 2:4–10)

> **Definition of Mercy:** Steadfast love. The Hebrew word for this is *hesed*. Although difficult to translate into English, *hesed* has the basic sense of that loving kindness, mercy, and faithfulness of God expressed in the act by which He chose Israel, established a covenant relationship with the people of Israel, promised them salvation, and bound Himself to loving them and showing them mercy. Those who have been called by grace into this covenant relationship with God respond in love to God and their fellow human beings.[3]

In the space below, write how God has shown mercy toward you in your life.

Faith is a gift from God. We cannot choose faith or develop it on our own. God plants it in us when we are baptized and when we read or hear His Word. We cannot stir up faith on our own.

Are you struggling with your faith right now? Ask God to strengthen your faith, and He will! Rest in the confidence of knowing that faith is a gift from the Holy Spirit.

Did you know you are a masterpiece? Think about how God has created you to be special and unique. Take some time to write these out; it might not be easy to write them out because sometimes we struggle to see the special things about ourselves.

- Read Ephesians 2:4–10 again, and list God's promises to you.
- God's grace covers every area of your life.

Discussion Question 16: In what areas of your life do you need to remember that God's grace covers you?

Write a prayer asking your Abba Father to help you remember that you are covered by God's grace.

Day 4: Nothing Can Separate You from Abba's Love

Thirty-five years later, I still remember her eyes—sad, lonely, with hope snuffed out. I met her when I volunteered to canvas a neighborhood and share the Gospel. "Do you know how much God loves you?" I asked from her front porch. She stood there with a baby in her arms. She was not much older than me, but all the cares of life had aged and worn heavily on her face. She looked at me with tears in her eyes and said, "I am not sure that I am good enough for God to love me." As gently as I could, I said, "God loves you unconditionally. You do not have to be good enough to earn His love." I know she heard my words, but I don't know if they reached her heart. She looked down, thanked me for stopping by, and closed the door.

Maybe her eyes haunt me because I sometimes fall into the trap of thinking I am not good enough. Maybe you do this too. We strive to be good, to do all that we are supposed to do and be as best as we can. And we falsely believe we must earn our way into our heavenly Father's good graces. Because our original parents—Adam and Eve—committed the original sin, none of us can stand before our perfect heavenly Father.

How can we make ourselves worthy?

We can't.

Are we then stuck in our sin?

We aren't.

God solved the problem for us. He sent His only Son, Jesus, to bear our punishment, take our place, and wear our shame.

Discussion Question 17: What causes you to wonder if you are enough?

56

When sin came into the world, it separated us from God. God is perfect and holy. Sin is an abomination to Him.

In the Garden of Eden, God promised He would send a Savior (see Genesis 3:15). Let's travel to the Garden of Gethsemane and see God's perfect love poured out for us. This is the first time we see God as Abba in Scripture.

> And they went to a place called Gethsemane. And He said to His disciples, "Sit here while I pray." And He took with Him Peter and James and John, and began to be greatly distressed and troubled. And He said to them, "My soul is very sorrowful, even to death. Remain here and watch." And going a little farther, He fell on the ground and prayed that, if it were possible, the hour might pass from Him. And He said, "Abba, Father, all things are possible for You. Remove this cup from Me. Yet not what I will, but what You will." (Mark 14:32–36)
>
> And being in agony He prayed more earnestly; and His sweat became like great drops of blood falling down to the ground. (Luke 22:44)

The anguish Jesus felt is beyond our understanding, but His love for us kept Him moving forward. Jesus knew the horror of what awaited Him. He went before the Father, asking if there was any other way. But there was none. Sin had entered the world through one man—Adam—so it had to be removed by one Man. Consider these points as we think about our Savior's suffering:

- His suffering was physical, emotional, and spiritual. The word *crucifixion* is related to the word *excruciating*; the physical pain would have caused immense suffering. Jesus had to bear the sin of the whole world upon Himself; He grieved for all humankind, especially those who do not believe. He was holy and without sin; He is true God, so He knew what lay ahead. But the most painful part was that Jesus had to suffer alone. Jesus willingly faced separation from God so you and I would never be separated from God.

- You will never suffer alone. Jesus, whose suffering is beyond anything we will ever bear, sits with you in your suffering and gives you His strength to pass through it.
- You can come before the almighty God and call Him *Abba* because you are His beloved child through your Baptism.
- Your sin no longer separates you from God; it has been removed from you. Your Abba holds you close to His heart and will never let you go.

The world will screech and scream and try to convince you that you are separated from God. Every day, we are bombarded by millions of messages through the media until our brains become overwhelmed, and we feel anxious. Why?

- We have lived through a global pandemic that threatens our health and that of our loved ones.
- We are enduring a gut-wrenching political division that imperils our nation.
- We are isolated by social media that does not provide the connection for which we long.

What causes you to feel separated from your heavenly Father?

Satan masterfully uses the things of this world, such as politics, illness, social media, and war, to gaslight our thoughts about ourselves and others and to put up a barrier between us and our Father in heaven. Satan loves to whisper, "Does God love you? Are you sure God will forgive all of your sins?" Satan will work through whatever means he can use to pull us away from the truth of God's love. The devil even causes our own guilt and shame to join in the unholy whispering, convincing us we are not enough.

Remember this precious truth: the Christian life is not based on a list of things we must do to be saved; it is based on what Jesus Christ did for us on the cross. God's love for us is not changed by how others see or feel about us or even about how we feel about ourselves.

> For you did not receive the spirit of slavery to fall back into fear, but you have received the Spirit of adoption as sons, by whom we cry, "Abba! Father!" (Romans 8:15)

Rest in these promises:

- There is nothing that can separate you from the love of God.
- God's love for you cannot be undone.

  No, in all these things we are more than conquerors through Him who loved us. For I am sure that neither death nor life, nor angels nor rulers, nor things present nor things to come, nor powers, nor height nor depth, nor anything else in all creation, will be able to separate us from the love of God in Christ Jesus our Lord. (Romans 8:37–39)

Do you know someone who seems separated from God? What is your prayer for that person?

Day 5: Circumstances You Did Not Choose

We've all faced circumstances we did not choose. I am sure none of us would ever choose to live through a pandemic, wildfires, hurricanes, flooding, and the aftermath of how the early months of this decade have impacted our lives.

Painful predicaments will plague us throughout life. We can count on it.

Discussion Question 18: What did you learn from dealing with the uncertainty of the last couple of years?

We cannot plan for every calamity and heartache, but our compassionate heavenly Father is with us in our troubles and gives us a way through.

Many years ago, I was engaged in a battle I did not choose. At first, it involved just my job, but soon the complexity of the problem permeated all areas of my life. How would I get through the challenge?

Trusted friends recommended a counselor who was also a pastor to help me navigate through the crisis. The counselor kept me buried in God's Word through Bible study and recommended helpful Christian books.

God surrounded me with His peace and lavished His grace upon me. His Word anchored my mind to His promises of forgiveness and salvation. The Holy Spirit comforted me with Scripture and strengthened my faith to face each moment. Jesus strengthened me by the gifts of the Lord's Supper and the daily gifts of my Baptism. And my weary heart found refuge in worship. I love that it is called the *Divine Service*. Abba Father met me there in the Word and Sacrament. I soaked it up like a dry sponge. Even when I was too broken to talk, I found comfort and peace in the rhythms and words of the Divine Service.

Worship isn't about what we do for God—attending a church service and making our offering. Worship is all about what Abba Father does for us. God, being present in the bread and wine, offers Himself to us. His pure grace flows to us, forgiving our sins and strengthening our hearts and souls to face whatever comes.

As I look back, I know Jesus held me close and held me up through that difficult situation. I received the Lord's Supper as often as I could. The nourishment I gained through Jesus' body and blood was more precious to me than any physical food or drink because it fed my soul and spirit.

> Sing to God, sing praises to His name; lift up a song to Him
> who rides through the deserts; His name is the LORD; exult
> before Him! Father of the fatherless and protector of widows
> is God in His holy habitation. (Psalm 68:4–5)

Have you ever been trapped in a circumstance you didn't choose or create? Reflect on it here.

You cannot solve, fix, or escape it. Emotional and mental oppression settles into all areas of your life like an uninvited guest, and you wonder if it will ever leave. And you look for help wherever it might be.

The world loves to offer up platitudes and wave them around like banners of truth when they are exactly the opposite. We do ourselves a disservice when we repeat platitudes such as "God helps those who help themselves." If I believed that lie, the battle would have destroyed me. There was nothing I could do to help myself during that terrible time. I had to walk through the difficult circumstance not knowing when or how it would end. Trusting Abba was all I had, and it was all I needed.

Here is another failed favorite: "God will never give you more than you can handle." God does not sit in heaven and say, "Let's see how she handles this crisis." Bad things happen because we live in a sinful and fallen world. Pandemics and wars. Political division and personal struggles. Natural disasters and accidents. We don't have to handle our problems on our own because God is with us. He is personal, present, and hands-on.

Problems, challenges, difficult people, divisions. Every single thing— big or small—that makes us cry, feel broken, or feel lonely can be laid at the foot of Christ's cross. Jesus took your burdens upon Himself at Calvary, and He faced them for you, my friend. And He resolved every sin that caused every problem.

God always meets us where we are, whether at our zenith or when rock meets bottom. He meets us in the place of despair. It doesn't matter whether we have been weakened by illness, a hopeless search for love, or a friend's betrayal. Jesus meets us in our suffering as the One who suffers with us.

READ PSALM 71

We don't know who wrote this psalm, but its author is clear about one thing: we can trust God. Our strength—mental, emotional, and physical—will fail, but God does not fail.

> Suffering isn't something to be sought after, yet in a profound way, suffering is something worth rejoicing over. When we're convinced that we don't have anything left, we have no choice but to depend on Jesus. When we give up our fight, we have no choice but to rely on Jesus to fight for us. When we realize we can't face something on our own, we have no choice but to finally trust that God can handle it.
>
> Jesus doesn't wait for you to get through the suffering. He meets you in the midst of it. Jesus doesn't back away from the suffering; He enters into the blood and the bruises and promises to listen to you when you feel like you've lost it all.[4]

READ MARK 14:36

Jesus knows better than we ever can that our life on earth will be one of torment and tumult. Here, we see Jesus crying out to His Father, confident in all that the Father can do for Him, and submitting to His will for Jesus and for humankind.

Discussion Question 19: How has Jesus met you in your suffering?

How can your previous experiences and the message of Psalm 71 guide you the next time you are in a difficult situation you did not choose?

Week 2 Group Study Questions

Abba

Abba: *The closest word for* Abba *in the English language is "Papa" or "Daddy."*

Pronunciation: *ab'-bah*

Abba *is used only three times in Scripture, but each instance points us to God as our Father. We have been adopted into God's family through Jesus.*

Bible Verse: *"See what kind of love the Father has given to us, that we should be called children of God; and so we are. The reason why the world does not know us is that it did not know Him." (1 John 3:1)*

REFLECTIONS

- Review Day 2 and Day 3 about the parable of the prodigal son.
- Read Luke 15:11–32.
- Spend time in class reflecting on the parable.
- What did you learn about God as Abba?
- What stories or Scripture do you want to remember from this week's lesson?

DISCUSSION QUESTIONS

11. What is or was your relationship with your earthly father? How has it affected how you see God as your Father?

12. What are some ways you can remember that God is your Abba Father daily? Here are a couple ideas to add to your own:
    - Make the sign of the cross when you wake up and when you go to bed to remember your Baptism and that you have been marked with the cross of Christ forever.
    - Pray the Lord's Prayer.

13. Do you try to hide your sin from God? Why or why not?

14. What would the Father say to you right now if you confessed your sins to Him and repented of them? How would He look at you?

15. To which of the sons in the parable of the prodigal son do you relate the most? Why?

16. In what areas of your life do you need to remember that God's grace covers you?

17. What causes you to wonder if you are enough?

18. What did you learn from dealing with the uncertainty of the last couple of years?

19. How has Jesus met you in your suffering?

BENEDICTION

The LORD bless you and keep you;
The LORD make His face to shine upon you and be gracious
to you;
The LORD lift up His countenance upon you and give you
peace. (Numbers 6:24–26)

El Roi

El Roi: *The God who sees me*

Pronunciation: *'ēl ro-ee'*

The only time this name of God is used in Scripture is in Genesis 16:13–14.

Bible Verse: *"So she called the name of the LORD who spoke to her, 'You are a God of seeing,' for she said, 'Truly here I have seen Him who looks after me.'" (Genesis 16:13)*

Day 1: Desperate Plans

As I study Hagar, Abram, and Sarai's lives, I see myself in each of them. Perhaps you will too. Before you begin today's lesson, ask God to show you what you need to know, hear, and see to better understand His character. God is with you in each moment, even when the Scriptures reveal something about yourself you wish wasn't true (which mostly has to do with our sinfulness and how we do not trust God above all things). Yet God loves you beyond all earthly reason. As the Creator of the universe, as your Creator and Lord, God sees you now and eternally.

GOD CALLED ABRAM

In Genesis 12:1–3, we read that God called Abram to leave his country, family, and home. God was asking Abram to give up his inheritance and identity. Abram's family worshiped false idols. At this point in Abram's story, we don't know what he even knew about the one true God—but God called him anyway.

Regardless of Abram's shortcomings, God commanded him to do His will and set him apart from other men. In Genesis 12, we see that God chose Abram not because of his achievements but because of God's plan for humankind's salvation. Above all, He is a loving and merciful God.

In these verses, God made six promises to Abram:

- God would make Abram a great nation.
- He would bless him.
- He would make his name great.
- He would bless those who bless Abram.
- He would curse those who curse him.
- He would bless all the families of the earth through Abram.

The first promise surely caused Abram and Sarai to pause because Sarai was barren (Genesis 11:30). They must have questioned how they could become a great nation without having children.

READ GENESIS 16

After a decade of waiting for God's promise to be fulfilled, Sarai suggested a plan to help God out. She offered her servant Hagar to become Abram's wife. Because Hagar was a slave belonging to Sarai, any child born to Hagar would belong to Sarai and Abram.

Discussion Question 20: What is the longest you have ever waited for something?

Have you ever taken a matter into your own hands because you were tired of waiting? Reflect on what happened.

Desperate plans do not fulfill our dreams—sometimes, they become our nightmares.

Abram did what Sarai asked, and Hagar became pregnant. Hagar did not have a choice in the matter. Can you imagine not having a say over any part of your life, even whom you marry? This might partly explain why Hagar treated Sarai with contempt. From Sarai's perspective, a slave had no rights—the slave's place was to do what she was told.

Sarai blamed Abram for Hagar's actions, even though he did what Sarai had requested of him. Hagar was sent back to Sarai to serve as a maid. Sarai mistreated Hagar, and she fled.

We are not surprised by the way this situation turned out, because we have the benefit of all of Scripture to help us put it into perspective. But perhaps we can understand Sarai's motivation. Sarai's plan was shortsighted and clouded by her yearning, but she ached for a baby. She saw the years slipping by without the child God had promised. Sarai doubted that God could make His promise happen. Or she may have thought she misunderstood God's words to Abram. Sarai's unchecked longing broke her heart and the hearts of those around her. Only God could mend the broken pieces back together.

GOD SAW HAGAR

The Angel of the Lord came to Hagar as she waited by a spring. He knew she was a servant of Sarai, and he called her by name. Still, he asked her where she came from and where she would go.

> **Angel of the Lord.** The Hebrew is *Mal'ak Yahweh*, "messenger of Yahweh." This special angel speaks on God's behalf, and from ancient days people have seen this as Christ before the incarnation. It makes sense, too, from a New Testament perspective. Jesus was and is and is to come. He has always been, and it makes sense that when God interacts in a physical form (even the pillar of fire and cloud) in His creation, this is the Son. This changes everything about how we read the Old Testament. Jesus came to Hagar. Jesus comes to us in our Baptism, the Holy Supper, and through His Word.

When Hagar answered that she was fleeing from her mistress, the angel told her to return and to submit to Sarai. He promised Hagar that her offspring would be many and that she would name her son *Ishmael*, which means "the Lord hears" (see verses 7–12). Take note:

- The Angel of the Lord is Jesus, appearing to her in human form.
- Jesus came to a servant girl; He knew her and called her by name (Genesis 16:8).
- Ishmael's name would forever be a reminder to her how God saw her affliction and answered her.
- Through Ishmael, her descendants would be many.
- Jesus walked into the brokenness of her story and gave her His promises.

HAGAR GAVE GOD A NAME

So she called the name of the LORD who spoke to her, "You are a God of seeing," for she said, "Truly here I have seen Him who looks after me." Therefore the well was called

Beer-lahai-roi; it lies between Kadesh and Bered. (Genesis 16:13–14)

Do you ever wonder why God chose certain stories to be in the Bible? Every detail we read shows us who He is and how He loves all His children.

Hagar, an Egyptian servant girl, gave God a name, and we are given front-row seats to this story. I wonder if perhaps He wants us to know He sees us, no matter our station in life. He not only sees us but also cares about every aspect of our circumstances.

Beer-lahai-roi means "the well of Him who lives and sees me." The people who visit the well would be reminded that God lives and sees them too.

In verses 15–16, Hagar gave birth to Ishmael. Sarai's name isn't mentioned. Ishmael was known as the son of Hagar and Abram, and his lineage is a fulfillment of God's covenant to give Abram many descendants.

Discussion Question 21: How have you ever felt unseen?

Feeling invisible is a lonely feeling. Perhaps, like Hagar, you didn't have a say in a circumstance in your life. God hears and sees you because you are His beloved child. He calls you precious and redeemed because of His Son, Jesus.

Maybe you felt like Sarai and waited for God to answer your prayer. Perhaps you doubted God's timing and His solutions because you viewed the situation from your viewpoint. Maybe you even thought God needed your help.

As we look at this story in Genesis, it can be hard to see how Sarai could not trust God, but we know the ending of the story. When we find ourselves stuck in a situation we did not anticipate, exhausted from trying to predict God's plan, we try to take matters into our own hands. We don't trust God, and so we play at being God with our feeble attempts to control our lives and those around us. This is a sin against the First Commandment; we are to fear, love, and trust God above all things, but we don't. We delude ourselves into thinking we have a better way. I have done this countless times. God understands our tendency toward this kind of temptation, yet His love for us doesn't change.

Friends, we not only know how Sarai's story turned out, but we know the end of our story too. God fulfilled His promises to her. And He has graciously given us what He promised in the garden—a Son who would make us into a great nation of His children. Jesus overcame every heartbreaking situation, and He fills the gap left in our lives by disappointment and unfulfilled desires. We are a community of believers now, and someday we will be in heaven with Him forever. For now, He promises to be with us always, and we can trust that He is our El Roi—the God who sees us.

Spend some time reflecting on this story and your own season of waiting. Maybe you are in the midst of it right now.

Sometimes, our stories feel painful and lonely, but I encourage you to remember that God sees you in your waiting and remains with you. May you find comfort in these words.

SCRIPTURE PRAYER

The eyes of the LORD are toward the righteous and His ears toward their cry. The face of the LORD is against those who do evil, to cut off the memory of them from the earth. When the righteous cry for help, the LORD hears and delivers them out of all their troubles. The LORD is near to the broken-hearted and saves the crushed in spirit. (Psalm 34:15–18)

BENEDICTION

The LORD bless you and keep you;
The LORD make His face to shine upon you and be gracious to you;
The LORD lift up His countenance upon you and give you peace. (Numbers 6:24–26)

Be in the presence of the One who sees you even when you feel unseen. You are held in the capable hands of the One who watches over you, today and always.

Day 2: El Roi Sees Your Heartache

Sitting at my desk, typing, I was surprised to see my boss poke his head into my office. He held a pamphlet in his hand, and he waved it at me. He chuckled, "Tomorrow I am going to a workshop about working with difficult people, so I can learn how to deal with you." Surprise at the insult filled my eyes, and before I could respond, he said, "Just kidding."

A deep sigh arose from my bruised heart. I knew my boss well enough to know he wasn't kidding. I squirmed in my chair trying to deal with the hurt, thinking for a moment that maybe there was something wrong with me. I wondered why he couldn't understand that people were different—each with their own strengths. It hurt that he saw me as an obstacle rather than someone to appreciate. A glimmer of hope began to grow as I thought about what he might learn at the seminar. Studying different personality types was something I loved to do. My confidence grew as I thought about all the ideas he would learn. I was hopeful that we could, together, improve our working relationship.

When he returned from the workshop, he called me into his office to take a personality test. It revealed we were exact opposites, which was no surprise to me. I was ready to roll up my sleeves and find the best way to work together despite our differences. Instead, my boss launched into a diatribe of how each of my personality traits was a problem instead of an asset. He ripped me to shreds. As he talked, I tried to remain composed, but I choked on my tears. When the cruel tirade was nearly over, he delivered the last blow: "You will always fail in life because you are too emotional."

Thankfully, it was time to leave for the day. I drove home in a fog. *What I was going to do?* I wanted to quit. Unfortunately, for various reasons, quitting was not an option. My heart ached as I thought about having to face my boss day after day.

Devastated, I called my parents. The soothing sound of their voices calmed me. Their encouragement filled me with determination and courage to face my boss again. I knew my parents were praying for me.

READ PSALM 34:12–18

Perhaps you have felt misunderstood or have even been bullied by a boss, friend, family member, or teacher. The ache burrows deep into your heart and stirs up your emotions. The sad reality is that on this side of heaven, we will experience anguish in our relationships, with those who know us well and with those who don't know us at all. All human relationships are subject to failure and pain.

So what can we do when we are stuck in a difficult situation like this? I encourage you to develop a list of Bible verses that bring you comfort and peace. These verses will become a landing place for you, a sacred space where you can meet with God. In His Word, He will remind you that He is not blind to your pain or uncaring. Rather, our compassionate Lord wraps you in His grace.

Here are a couple of my favorites:

> The LORD your God is in your midst, a mighty one who will save; He will rejoice over you with gladness; He will quiet you by His love; He will exult over you with loud singing. (Zephaniah 3:17)

> But as for me, I will look to the LORD; I will wait for the God of my salvation; my God will hear me. Rejoice not over me, O my enemy; when I fall, I shall rise; when I sit in darkness, the LORD will be a light to me. (Micah 7:7–8)

Discussion Question 22: What Bible passages bring you comfort? Why?

Discussion Question 23: Like Hagar, maybe you have found yourself in a circumstance you didn't choose. What was it? How did you handle it?

I would have chosen never to work with a boss who crushed my self-esteem. To him, I was always wrong. My job didn't get easier, because

I couldn't live up to his expectations. But in the evening hours, I immersed myself in reading the Bible, brought it all before God in prayer, and determined to internalize what God was teaching me in this situation.

One day, I asked for time off to attend my brother's graduation. I explained that I was ahead of schedule with my responsibilities related to a big project at work. I showed my boss documentation regarding how I had worked to ensure my absence would not hamper the project. He said I couldn't go, and if I did, the consequences would be severe.

You might wonder why I stayed? I had made a commitment to stay for a year and was compelled to see it through. For the same reason, because it was a formal commitment, my boss was forced to keep me on the job. In addition, I couldn't afford to quit; it wasn't an option at that time. Missing my brother's graduation broke my heart, but the kind actions of family and friends helped me get through it. On the day of my brother's graduation, my family sent me a beautiful bouquet, and a wonderful friend traveled several hours to spend the evening with me. I believe that such kindnesses are extensions of God's love for us. Showing love and affection is a way we live out our vocations as family members and friends.

What can you do when hurt settles into your soul? Bitterness can spread like wildfire, destroying your peace. Jesus promises that we can pray about anything (see, for example, Philippians 4:6; Mark 11:24; John 15:7; Luke 11:9). When you feel bitterness threatening to consume you, pray in Jesus' name about the hurt in your heart and ask that God give you His peace.

Sometimes we need extra help and guidance to sort through complicated relationships. There is no shame in talking to a trusted pastor or finding a Christian counselor. I am thankful for the time I have spent with counselors. I was able to navigate through troubling circumstances with their support and guidance. With their help, God mended my broken heart, enabling me to forgive.

READ COLOSSIANS 3:12—17

Life doesn't always go the way we plan. It is tempting to become fearful or angry when we don't know the future, because life is uncertain; however, such emotions aren't healthy or helpful. As I write this, we all have faced the myriad challenges of 2020 and 2021 that seemed to bring new difficulties every day. Some of us endured months of uncertainty, not knowing when life would return to normal. I remember feeling anxiety crouching in the corners of my mind; the predictability I once enjoyed was gone. But here is the precious truth: the Lord goes before us each day, week, month, season, year, and decade. He promises to work all things—even bad things—to the good of those who love Him. We can count on that.

What causes you to feel uncertain?

I talk with women around the world, listen to their stories, and try to help them put their circumstances into the bigger picture of God's will for them. Many of them have faced challenges they didn't choose, but as they sorted through the broken pieces of their lives, many could see how Jesus brought them through the tough times. Even in their loneliest and darkest hours, they were always in the presence of El Roi, who sees the bigger picture and knows His will for them.

Because God is faithful, because He turns all things into good for the benefit of those who love Him, we can trust that every trouble will be turned to something good. Reflect on a time you have seen this in your own life.

Day 3: El Roi Sees Your Tears

THE STORY OF HAGAR CONTINUES

We are jumping ahead to Genesis 21 for more of Hagar's story. In Week 4, we will return to Genesis 17, in which God gives Abram and Sarai new names and they learn they are pregnant with Isaac. In this session, though, we continue our study of the name *El Roi*, which Hagar used for God.

> And the child grew and was weaned. And Abraham made a great feast on the day that Isaac was weaned. But Sarah saw the son of Hagar the Egyptian, whom she had borne to Abraham, laughing. So she said to Abraham, "Cast out this slave woman with her son, for the son of this slave woman shall not be heir with my son Isaac." And the thing was very displeasing to Abraham on account of his son. But God said to Abraham, "Be not displeased because of the boy and because of your slave woman. Whatever Sarah says to you, do as she tells you, for through Isaac shall your offspring be named. And I will make a nation of the son of the slave woman also, because he is your offspring." (Genesis 21:8–13)

In those days, Jewish women usually nursed their children until they were about three years old. Isaac would have been about three and Ishmael about fourteen years old. We do not know why Ishmael laughed at Isaac, but I speculate that the antics of a three-year-old would cause a young man to laugh. Or maybe Ishmael, of whom God's angel says, "He shall be a wild donkey of a man" (Genesis 16:12), was just behaving as he typically did. Regardless, Ishmael laughed, and it got him and his mother banished.

As I look at this story, my heart goes out to Ishmael. As we discussed in the previous session, Sarah had taken matters into her own hands when she couldn't see how God would be able to fulfill His promise. The result was Ishmael. Sarah's solution was a reminder of her empty arms and the emptiness of her heart, as she watched Abraham's love grow for a child who was not hers.

What had been done couldn't be undone. Again, fear and jealousy stirred in Sarah's heart. She didn't want Ishmael around because she didn't want him to receive the firstborn privileges—she wanted those for Isaac.

Isaac was the fulfillment of God's covenant with Abraham and all it entailed. Nothing could remove the promise, yet we find Sarah stewing about it, again taking matters into her own hands by ordering Hagar to leave.

Discussion Question 24: What is your Ishmael—a problem you have taken into your own hands?

We all have the impulse to take the reins and devise our own solutions to problems. In some cases, however, we don't fix things; we make them worse. Abraham grieved over what Sarah asked him to do. How could Abraham let go of Ishmael? God reminded him of the covenant He had made in Genesis 17—Ishmael would become a great nation because he, too, was Abraham's son.

Discussion Question 25: Are you surprised by God's tenderness toward Abraham? Why or why not?

God could have said to Abraham, "See what you did all those years ago, when you took matters into your own hands? You are on your own, buddy." Instead, God again lovingly reminded Abraham of His promises.

READ GENESIS 21:14–19

Letting go must have been extremely painful for all of them. But Abraham knew God would keep His promises, so he trusted God through the pain. He had the proof in his son Isaac, after all.

And again El Roi heard the cry of Hagar, and He spoke to her. He assured her that Ishmael would become a great nation. He offered her hope and comfort. Notice in verse 19 how El Roi opened her eyes so she could see the well. Grief and fear blinded Hagar from seeing it.

What is blinding you from identifying the gifts God has promised you? Ask God to show you what you need to see.

> And God was with the boy, and he grew up. He lived in the wilderness and became an expert with the bow. He lived in the wilderness of Paran, and his mother took a wife for him from the land of Egypt. (Genesis 21:20–21)

Do you see God's grace spilling over in these verses? God took the broken pieces caused when Abraham and Sarah did not trust His promises, and He fixed them. He watched over Ishmael and kept His promise to Abraham through Ishmael as well as through Isaac.

Maybe you identify more with Ishmael's character—caught up in a story you didn't write. Take heart and remember that, like Ishmael, God will never abandon you. He sees your tears. There have been times in my life when I thought God only wanted to hear edited versions of my troubles. I felt ashamed of how I felt, so I only presented details I thought would be the most pleasing to God. But it never felt genuine. My sorrow was the part I needed to share with Him the most, but I was afraid it would be too much for Him. Have you heard of a lament? It's a passionate expression of sorrow; as a prayer, a lament is pouring your heart out before God.

READ PSALM 56:8—11

Our almighty Creator, who sees everything and knows our every weakness, welcomes all our prayers, even the tearful ones. El Roi's love for us is not fickle. His love is constant and is strong enough to handle all our pain.

God collects your tears.

How have today's lesson and readings helped you let go of sorrow over a situation which you had no control of?

Day 4: You Are Never Alone

Thump! Thump! Thump! Echoes reverberated in the stairwell as I dragged my suitcase down the steps to my basement apartment.

I immediately saw the note from my landlord on my door—this was long before cell phones—to call my pastor as soon as possible. Unusual but not alarming. I dropped my bags and grabbed the phone. No answer. I left a message on his answering machine and hoped he would call me soon.

My luggage reminded me of the laundry I needed to take care of, but the couch looked better after several sleepless nights at a youth event. I dropped to the couch and called my mom to let her know I was home. But I was so startled to hear my sister's voice on the line that I almost dropped the phone. Jimella wasn't supposed to be at our parents' house; she should have been at the camp where she was a counselor.

Her voice quivered. "Have you talked to Pastor yet?"

I replied, "I called, but there was no answer."

Jimella told me my best friend's dad had been killed in a plane crash. The shock of the news was interspersed with memories of all the times spent at their house. He'd always treated me like a member of their family.

I wanted to be with my friend Deann, to go to her house and grieve with the family that was as close to me as my own. But reality hit me like a bucket of ice. *I can't go.* I had just started a new job and hadn't yet earned paid time off. I wouldn't be able to make the seven-hour drive home for the funeral.

I called Deann, and we cried together, remembering her dad. Then I spent the next couple of hours calling family and friends, trying to ease the ache in my heart. But each time the phone sat silent, loneliness returned.

My pastor stopped by and apologized for not being able to deliver the news to me in person as my mom had requested (she didn't want me to be alone when I learned about the crash). He prayed with me and asked if I would be okay. I had been at this church for only a few weeks, and I didn't know anyone very well. The congregation was friendly, but I missed the close connection of family and friends.

I was so tired; I needed to sleep. Tears soaked my pillow as I fell asleep. Around 3:00 a.m., I woke with a headache and the anguish of being alone. Thoughts of calling my grandma flitted through my mind; I knew she would be awake. Sniffing back another sob, I decided not to call, knowing the ache would still be there after I hung up the phone. Instead, I grabbed my Bible from the bedside table and opened it to Psalm 62. My soul soaked up the words.

> For God alone, O my soul, wait in silence, for my hope is
> from Him. He only is my rock and my salvation, my fortress;
> I shall not be shaken. On God rests my salvation and my
> glory; my mighty rock, my refuge is God. Trust in Him at all
> times, O people; pour out your heart before Him; God is a
> refuge for us. (Psalm 62:5–8)

The realization hit me—I wasn't alone or ignored. El Roi was with me. He saw my loneliness and heartache, just as He saw the grief of Deann and her family. As I knelt beside my bed with my Bible open, I prayed the psalm, and the peace of God's presence filled the room. Family and friends are a gift, but they cannot bring the peace that surpasses all human understanding, which is only found in Christ Jesus.

Where do you go to find comfort?

God knows you and loves you. Let that truth sink into your soul.

For the rest of this week, we will reflect and journal our way through Psalm 139. Reflection looks different for everyone: some will pause and think about it, and others will want to journal their way through. I encourage you to do what works best for you.

> O LORD, You have searched me and known me! (Psalm
> 139:1)

Discussion Question 26: The Lord knows every detail about you. How does it make you feel to remember God knows everything about you? Are there details you wish God didn't know?

Bring your faults and flaws before God. Take the time to write them out. When you are finished, rip them up, burn them, shred them, or throw them in the trash. This is a physical and visible way to release them and prayerfully hand them over to God. (This might be an activity you do later, if you don't have time to do it now.)

> You know when I sit down and when I rise up; You discern
> my thoughts from afar. (Psalm 139:2)

Do you struggle with your thoughts? Does your thinking derail your sleep and your peace? Bring each thought before God. He isn't surprised or mad at your thoughts, even the sinful ones. But God does want each of us to confess our sins and repent of them. We can be comfortable doing this because God promises us forgiveness that Jesus earned for us on the cross. So examine your sins and ask God to reshape the way you view your challenges. However, if you find yourself struggling with a vexing sin, talk with your pastor and consider private confession and absolution. Pastors are uniquely trained to listen and respond with the comfort of the Gospel of Jesus Christ.

List as many thoughts in your journal or in the space opposite as you like. Don't judge or edit them. Simply write them as they come to you, and let God help you navigate through them. This could become a daily practice, in which you bring your thoughts before the Lord.

> You search out my path and my lying down and are
> acquainted with all my ways. (Psalm 139:3)

God is aware of how you spend your time. List some of the ways you spend your time in the space below. As you have time, color the clock at the beginning of this chapter and consider how you spend your discretionary time.

> Even before a word is on my tongue, behold, O LORD, You
> know it altogether. (Psalm 139:4)

God knows you so well—He knows what you are going to say before you say it. What did you think when you read that? Think about the words you speak—the good and the bad.

How might God help you with your words?

> You hem me in, behind and before, and lay Your hand upon
> me. Such knowledge is too wonderful for me; it is high; I
> cannot attain it. (Psalm 139:5–6)

Do you wonder or worry about the future? Take comfort in knowing that God goes before you.

What are your concerns about the future? Write them here, and put them in God's hands.

Which verses of the psalm were most meaningful to you? Why?

Day 5: The Shelter of His Presence

Where shall I go from Your Spirit? Or where shall I flee from Your presence? If I ascend to heaven, You are there! If I make my bed in Sheol, You are there! If I take the wings of the morning and dwell in the uttermost parts of the sea, even there Your hand shall lead me, and Your right hand shall hold me. (Psalm 139:7–10)

God is always with you, even in seemingly mundane, everyday tasks. Spend some time thinking about the routines of your day and list them here. As you write them, think about how God meets you in each moment. Remember He loves you and is passionate about all areas of your life—the magnificent and dull.

When I _____, I am loved by God.

_____, I am loved by God.

_____, I am loved by God.

_____, I am loved by God.

As I _____, I am loved by God.

_____, I am loved by God.

_____, I am loved by God.

_____, I am loved by God.

We all are a little like Hagar, because we all know what it is like to endure circumstances we did not choose. You may encounter painful memories when you reflect on this. Be assured that even in moments of loneliness, God was there with you; He never left your side.

Maybe you are navigating through a difficult time right now. El Roi sees you and understands your struggle. But He isn't a distant observer.

God the Son endured all of the same things you are experiencing right now—pain, fatigue, sorrow, anxiety, loneliness. He meets you where you are, giving His strength to you as He holds you in His hands. Your compassionate Lord comes to you through His Word and in the Lord's Supper, renewing and strengthening your faith.

Discussion Question 27: What is the darkest day you have experienced in your life so far?

> If I say, "Surely the darkness shall cover me, and the light
> about me be night," even the darkness is not dark to You; the
> night is bright as the day, for darkness is as light with You.
> (Psalm 139:11–12)

At times, darkness seems to cover our days, and we feel overwhelmed. We wonder how we can deal with such moments and come out the other side. But God never leaves us to our own devices, alone in the darkness without a light. Let's illustrate this. In your mind (or literally, if you can), go into a room that has no light. Total blackness fills the room. You cannot see your hand in front of your face. Now, light a candle. The light repels the darkness. Think about some dark moments you have faced or are currently facing, and ask God to help you remember that His light is always shining. The darkness cannot overcome the light. Jesus is the light of the world.

> For You formed my inward parts; You knitted me together in
> my mother's womb. I praise You, for I am fearfully and won-
> derfully made. Wonderful are Your works; my soul knows it
> very well. My frame was not hidden from You, when I was
> being made in secret, intricately woven in the depths of the
> earth. Your eyes saw my unformed substance; in Your book
> were written, every one of them, the days that were formed
> for me, when as yet there was none of them. How precious to
> me are Your thoughts, O God! How vast is the sum of them!
> If I would count them, they are more than the sand. I awake,
> and I am still with You. (Psalm 139:13–18)

The Hebrew word for "intricately woven" is "embroidered." You are God's masterpiece! Your Creator sees every tiny aspect of who you are and every millisecond of your life. Nothing is hidden from El Roi.

When was the last time you thought about yourself as a precious treasure? Do you believe you are a masterpiece? Why or why not?

We don't often think of ourselves as precious, because it is easier to focus on our faults and the challenges of our lives. But God calls us His work of art.

Color the page at the beginning of this chapter when you have time. You are a one-of-a-kind miracle, fashioned and created by the God of the universe.

> God saw us when we could not be seen, and he wrote about us when there was nothing of us to write about.[5]

God continues to see you, even when it feels like no one else does.

> Oh that You would slay the wicked, O God! O men of blood, depart from me! They speak against You with malicious intent; Your enemies take Your name in vain. Do I not hate those who hate You, O LORD? And do I not loathe those who rise up against You? I hate them with complete hatred; I count them my enemies. (Psalm 139:19–22)

Have you ever found yourself in a situation in which you felt powerless to affect the outcome? Such circumstances can make you feel insignificant. You feel helpless. You may wonder why God doesn't stop it. It may seem like evil is winning.

When I was growing up, my dad would say, "It's important to remember that we live in a sick and sinful world, but God is always good. God is always in control, even when you cannot see it. God knows and sees what you are going through, and He will never abandon you."

One of the most helpless times in our recent history was September 11, 2001. I will never forget the feelings I had that day. I felt physically ill as I watched the towers come down. My heart hurt as I watched the news, and I became distressed. Finally, Troy and I decided we could not continue watching the news coverage. We looked instead to the only One, Jesus, who could lead us through those moments in history. Since that time we've learned to turn off the news and remember what God has done and is doing for us.

During the pandemic, when we felt overwhelmed, we listed the ways God has helped us in the past. God's peace surrounded us as we recalled how His mercy sustained us when we felt hopeless. The problems remained, but we didn't focus on them. We firmly fixed our eyes on Jesus (see Hebrews 12:2).

The Bible is filled with the history of God's provision and protection in troubled times. He delivered the children of Israel through the Red Sea and across the wilderness. He preserved the firstborn sons of the Jews when Pharaoh wouldn't heed Moses' warning and again when Herod was determined to slay the new King. He delivered His people from lions, fire, storms, and murderers. And He helps you in every trouble, every heartache. Rest in the shelter of God's grace. El Roi sees you and will faithfully walk beside you.

Discussion Question 28: How has God been with you in the past? How were His compassion and provision manifested in that situation?

If it is difficult to think of any examples, you can start with how God rescued you from sin. On your own, you could have never saved yourself, but God sent His Son, Jesus, to rescue you.

> Search me, O God, and know my heart! Try me and know
> my thoughts! And see if there be any grievous way in me,
> and lead me in the way everlasting! (Psalm 139:23–24)

We often want to cover up who we are before God. We are like Adam and Eve in the garden; once they realized they were sinful and naked, they tried to hide from God. But they could not hide from Him. The Lord came to them to show them their sin and to help them understand the source of it. And He came with a covenant: the promise of a Savior who would crush all sin.

In the garden, God also gave Adam and Eve garments to cover their nakedness to protect them from the elements that they now had to live with. These garments are forerunners of the robes of righteousness that our Savior wraps around us in our Baptism. God covered Adam and Eve's vulnerability, and Christ Jesus covers our vulnerability with His grace.

I encourage you to examine yourself by asking God to search your heart, thoughts, and mind and reveal your sins to you. As you do this, remember who God is and who you are as His child:

- He is Elohim, who breathed into you the breath of life. He knows you and calls you by name.
- He is your Abba Father who runs toward you, and He loves you beyond measure.
- He is El Roi—the God who sees you always. Not even your friends, spouse, siblings, or parents know you as well as God knows you. He knows everything about you, the things you want people to know and the things you hope no one ever discovers. He loves you.
- God is a kind and faithful companion who will not abandon you or look away as you confront your sins—the ones you are already aware of and the ones He brings to light. The Law shows us our sins, and God, in His mercy, forgives us and removes them from us.
- He makes you His own beloved child in Baptism. He washes away your sins daily, removing them from you completely.

If shame is casting a shadow over you because you feel bad about a certain sin, ask God to help you move through it. Confess your sin, and then repent of it. God asks you to do this, and remember that when you do, He doesn't turn away from you. He turns toward you and reminds you of who you are. He will give you His strength and remind you that this sin has already been defeated on Calvary's cross. Your sin doesn't have the final say over who you are—God does, and He says, "I love you. You are Mine."

Discussion Question 29: What are your favorite verses from Psalm 139? Read the psalm as a group, and if you have time, talk about the journaling exercises.

Be with your heavenly Father, who turns His face toward you. Dwell with Him in His Word, and receive His gifts of forgiveness and grace.

WEEK 3 GROUP STUDY QUESTIONS

EL ROI

El Roi: *The God who sees me*

Pronunciation: *'ĕl ro-ee'*

The only time this name of God is used in Scripture is in Genesis 16:13–14.

Bible Verse: *"So she called the name of the LORD who spoke to her, 'You are a God of seeing,' for she said, 'Truly here I have seen Him who looks after me.'" (Genesis 16:13)*

REFLECTIONS

- What story stood out to you the most from this week's sessions? Why?
- What did you learn about God as El Roi?
- Review the story of Hagar from Genesis 16.

DISCUSSION QUESTIONS

20. What is the longest you have ever waited for something?

21. How have you ever felt unseen?

22. What Bible passages bring you comfort? Why?

23. Like Hagar, maybe you have found yourself in a circumstance you didn't choose. What was it? How did you handle it?

24. What is your Ishmael—a problem you have taken into your own hands?

25. Are you surprised by God's tenderness toward Abraham? Why or why not?

26. The Lord knows every detail about you. How does it make you feel to remember God knows everything about you? Are there details you wish God didn't know?

27. What is the darkest day you have experienced in your life so far?

28. How has God been with you in the past? How were His compassion and provision manifested in that situation?

29. What are your favorite verses from Psalm 139? Read the psalm as a group, and if you have time, talk about the journaling exercises.

BENEDICTION

The LORD bless you and keep you;
The LORD make His face to shine upon you and be gracious to you;
The LORD lift up His countenance upon you and give you peace. (Numbers 6:24–26)

El Shaddai

El (God) Shaddai: *Sustainer, all-sufficient*

Pronunciation: *ʾĕl shad-dahʾ-ee*

El Shaddai is mentioned forty-eight times in the Bible; the Book of Job mentions El Shaddai thirty-one times alone. Job's story deals with heartbreaking loss. El Shaddai strengthened him with His sufficiency to continue. From his story, we see that God is present with us and that His peace cannot be taken away from us. Martin Luther said "this name indicates the might and power of God. . . . He alone . . . has power over everything, needs no one's help, and is able to give all things to all."

Bible Verse: *"He who dwells in the shelter of the Most High will abide in the shadow of the Almighty." (Psalm 91:1)*

Day 1: Sustained in Sorrow

I sat because suddenly the room was spinning. I knew Grandma Katherine hadn't been feeling well, but the news that she had pancreatic cancer filled me with sadness and dread. She was the hub of our family. We all gravitated to her, and her love for her family members wrapped around us like the beautiful afghans she crocheted and gave as gifts. I felt especially close to her; she wrote letters to me weekly and was always available to talk on the phone.

"Oh, Mom," I said. "I just can't comprehend this. I'm so sorry!"

Mom replied with more bad news: "The cancer has metastasized to the areas around her pancreas. She's being admitted to the hospital to see if anything can be done."

"The chances of her surviving this are not good," I whispered softly.

She sighed, "No. The chances are not good. Grandma is in God's hands now." Mom promised to keep me updated, and we said goodbye.

I raged at God. My grandmother had already suffered through cancer twice—why a third time? Like a toddler, I cried out to God in a tangled, jumbled prayer: "Why, God? Why?"

A few days and four hundred miles later, I joined my family in Grandma's hospital room. As we talked, a lifetime of memories filled the room—a collection of bitter and sweet moments mingled with love and sadness. El Shaddai held my family together and covered us with the peace of His presence as we remembered God's promises to us in His Word.

The next day, Mom said, "There isn't anything more they can do. The cancer is too advanced. They will send her home and provide measures to make her comfortable. She could live a few more weeks or even months."

I hugged my mom, and we wept. I pulled myself together, determined to enjoy every moment with Grandma.

As I got ready for bed that night, anxious thoughts swirled through my mind. I knew I wouldn't be able to make another trip to see Grandma; the distance was too great. I knew this would be my last opportunity to say all the things I wanted to say to her this side of heaven. I struggled to strategize how I could ever say goodbye to a person who was so dear to me.

What am I going to do?

What if I say something by mistake that upsets her?

What if I cry? Will that make her cry too?

As I agonized with what words to say, I remembered Grandma's favorite Scripture passage, Psalm 91. She prayed those words daily for her loved ones.

> He who dwells in the shelter of the Most High will abide in
> the shadow of the Almighty. (Psalm 91:1)

I prayed God's Word, and El Shaddai strengthened my heart to face what felt impossible. The Almighty came near to my shattered soul and reminded me how much He loved my grandma—more than all my family combined. He would walk me through the valley of the shadow of death, and He would walk my grandma home to heaven. He reminded me I didn't need to fear what came next, because I was in the presence of El Shaddai.

I fell asleep that night in the peace of His presence, pouring my heart out before the Almighty and resting in His love.

Walking into Grandma's room the next day, I took a deep breath and remembered I was God's daughter and so was she. I felt secure in the promise that El Shaddai would care for both of us. His shadow provided a place of comfort and peace as I prepared to say goodbye.

Smiling and choking back tears, I reached out to hold Grandma's hands—a tender symbol of our relationship. She was always there to support, listen, pray, and encourage. Those hands had written hundreds of letters and cards to me over the years, each one filled with the love only a grandmother could give.

We laughed—Grandma had the best sense of humor. We enjoyed each other's presence. We loved each other, and all too soon, it was time for me to leave. El Shaddai gave me His strength to walk out of the room.

Grandma lived a few more months, and during that time, I wrote her long letters and talked with her on the phone. Each time, I told her how much she meant to me. I thanked her for being the best grandma and for all the time she spent listening to me. She said, "Michelle, I would do it all over again."

It has been over eighteen years since that day in Grandma's hospital room. I still cry when I revisit those precious memories. The love she gave will never fade, and I look forward to spending eternity with her in heaven. Remembering her reminds me how El Shaddai has helped me through every heartbreak.

It's important to remember stories in our own lives of how God has helped us so we can face what comes next. El Shaddai invites us to the only place we can find peace and confidence—His presence.

READ PSALM 91

These are some promises from El Shaddai to you in this psalm:

- God is your refuge and fortress.
- You can rest in His protection.
- His faithfulness is your shield.
- He is your dwelling place.
- He holds fast to you in love.

List the promises you see.

Discussion Question 30: What does *abide* mean to you?

Discussion Question 31: How does knowing God as El Shaddai help you?

SCRIPTURE PRAYER

He who dwells in the shelter of the Most High will abide
in the shadow of the Almighty. I will say to the LORD, "My
refuge and my fortress, my God, in whom I trust." (Psalm
91:1–2)

BENEDICTION

The LORD bless you and keep you;
The LORD make His face to shine upon you and be gracious
to you;
The LORD lift up His countenance upon you and give you
peace. (Numbers 6:24–26)

*Be in the presence of El Shaddai, who strengthens you with His sufficiency.
When you feel weak, remember you never face one moment alone. Rest in
the grace and peace of El Shaddai's presence.*

DAY 2: EL SHADDAI IS SUFFICIENT

The name *El Shaddai* is used first in Abraham's story. Between chapters 16 and 17 in Genesis, thirteen years have passed since Abram and Sarai tried to expedite God's promise through the birth of Ishmael.

> When Abram was ninety-nine years old the LORD appeared
> to Abram and said to him, "I am God Almighty; walk before
> Me, and be blameless, that I may make My covenant between
> Me and you, and may multiply you greatly." (Genesis 17:1–2)

Let's step into Abram's dusty sandals and imagine what it must have been like for him to see God face-to-face. Twenty-four years had passed from the time God promised Abram to one day make him a great nation. Ishmael grew into a young man.

READ GENESIS 17:18–21

One can assume from these verses that Abram is fond of his son and may have grown comfortable with the idea that perhaps Ishmael was the son of the promise after all. He and Sarai were well past child-bearing age. It was unthinkable, at that point, to believe they would be able to have a child of their own.

Abram has never heard God called El Shaddai before; God reveals to Abram who He is through His name. "In short, this name indicates the might and power of God. It means that He alone is powerful, is all-sufficient of Himself, has power over everything, needs no one's help, and is able to give all things to all."[6]

What does the name El Shaddai *reveal to you? How does knowing God is almighty and sufficient help you face your circumstances?*

Look at Abram's response to God's covenant:

> Then Abram fell on his face. And God said to him, "Behold,
> My covenant is with you, and you shall be the father of a
> multitude of nations. No longer shall your name be called
> Abram, but your name shall be Abraham, for I have made
> you the father of a multitude of nations. I will make you
> exceedingly fruitful, and I will make you into nations, and
> kings shall come from you. (Genesis 17:3–6)

Oh, friend, can you picture the scene? Abraham falls in worship before the God who walked with him all those years. God invited him to watch what He would do. Even the things that seemed impossible to human understanding were made possible by God's might.

To mark this covenant, God gives Abram a new name—*Abraham*, which means, "the father of the nations." The name is the promise.

Did you know God gives you a new name in His covenant with you through Holy Baptism? "My beloved child." Your name—*Christian*—reveals the promises God has given to you:

- You are His child.
- You are His beloved.
- You belong to Him.

> And I will establish My covenant between Me and you and
> your offspring after you throughout their generations for an
> everlasting covenant, to be God to you and to your offspring
> after you. And I will give to you and to your offspring after
> you the land of your sojournings, all the land of Canaan, for
> an everlasting possession, and I will be their God. (Genesis
> 17:7–9)

Go to this passage in your Bible and underline the verses. This is God's promise to all of us. He promises to love us in and through all things. You are a part of the covenant because Abraham is your father too.

READ GENESIS 17:9–14

What does God tell Abraham to do?

Other cultures practiced circumcision, but typically, Jewish males were circumcised at puberty to prepare them for marriage. In Egypt, circumcision was required for a man to enter the priesthood. But here, God made circumcision a part of the covenant between Him and His chosen people. God wanted all males, starting with infants eight days and older, to be circumcised. The covenant was connected to the outward act of circumcision.

> By removal of the foreskin, males received a visible sign (v
> 11) of God's promise to send a Savior, born of the woman
> (Galatians 4:4–5). No Hebrew male could live a day without
> being reminded of the promise God had made long before,
> and every conjugal act between a husband and wife would
> illustrate the hope that God was working to restore creation
> and redeem all people. Finally, the shedding of blood pointed
> to our final redemption by the shedding of Christ's blood.[7]

Therefore, through Abraham comes the promised Messiah, the Savior who would shed His blood for our sins. Jesus was circumcised when He was eight days old. He was the One to whom the covenant pointed and by whom the covenant was fulfilled.

God replaced the old covenant with the new one—Baptism. Physical circumcision is no longer required as a sign of our covenant with God.

> In Him also you were circumcised with a circumcision made
> without hands, by putting off the body of the flesh, by the
> circumcision of Christ, having been buried with Him in baptism, in which you were also raised with Him through faith
> in the powerful working of God, who raised Him from the
> dead. (Colossians 2:11–12)

READ TITUS 3:5—7

The same powerful working of God that raised Jesus from
the dead is at work in Baptism. Baptism puts to death the
sinful nature (Romans 6:6) and resurrects us in faith to a new
life in Christ. Baptism is not just a symbol of what God does
through the teaching of God's Word. It is water combined

with God's Word that makes it a washing of regeneration
(Titus 3:5–7).[8]

Regeneration means "to be born again, restored, renewed, completely made over. Regeneration is an act of God the Holy Spirit who works
through Word and Sacraments to bring a sinful, self-centered person into
union with Christ Jesus through faith (John 1:13, 3:1–12, 1 Peter 1:23)."[9]

El Shaddai calls to you through the waters of Holy Baptism and restores you to Himself. You are made new through the water and the Word.

Baptism is always about what God does for us. It is a gift He gives to us;
one we can't earn and don't deserve. Baptism is God's power at work in and
through us by means of the water and the Word.

El Shaddai's grace is sufficient. Take some time to look at your life
through the lens of what God gives you daily through Baptism:

- Your sins are forgiven and removed from you.
- God chose you as His own. You are His beloved child.
- God's grace covers you every moment.
- The Holy Spirit is within you and sustains your faith.

Through Baptism, God supplies all we need to face each day.

Discussion Question 32: Do you remember your Baptism? Do you
know your baptismal birthday? How has remembering your Baptism
encouraged you?

Discussion Question 33: How might remembering Abraham's story
encourage your faith?

How would you describe the name El Shaddai *in your own words?*

While reading a blog post by my friend Katie Koplin about remembering her Baptism, I was inspired by this quote: "When you wash your face,
remember your Baptism" (Martin Luther). Katie went on to say more that
grabbed my attention.

> I don't remember the details of my Baptism. I don't know
> what I was wearing, what the temperature was outside. I was
> too young to know what that Sunday morning looked like.

What I do know and can remember and dwell upon is what happened because of that water and because of those words. All of these good gifts are because of Jesus and in spite of me . . . yet for me. (How beautiful is that.)

If you can't remember the weather of the day, your outfit, or how the water felt, think on these things when you wash your face:

- Buried with Christ and raised with Him
- Made alive
- Canceled debt
- Clothed in Christ
- Walking in newness of life
- Death no longer has dominion
- Dead to sin and alive to God in Christ Jesus

All of these things are yours in spite of you and because of Christ.[10]

You are El Shaddai's beloved. Rest in His promises and the peace of His presence.

DAY 3: IMPOSSIBLE MADE POSSIBLE

READ GENESIS 17:15–17

What is Abraham's response to God?

Picture ninety-nine-year-old Abraham falling on his face again and laughing. In my mind's eye, I see joy, delight, and wonder. Some may think Abraham's behavior is disrespectful to God, but I don't think El Shaddai was mad or dismayed by his response. God knew He was about to make possible what was physically impossible. In His time and according to His plan, Abraham and Sarah conceived. All of creation would know that El Shaddai faithfully accomplished this great miracle.

In this passage, we also see God giving Sarai a new name. Within her name is the promise that she would be the mother of many nations. And even though Abraham and Sarah had forgotten God's covenant with them, God did not forget or change His mind.

We also forget God's promises. Our culture of individual success and independence distracts us from our dependence on God. Even so, El Shaddai will never remove His promises from us. He won't change His mind about us, because He loves us and is faithful to us. He strengthens us to face what seems impossible.

When I sent my oldest son off to college, I did not know how to do it with grace. A few months earlier, on the morning of his high school graduation party, I sat in church and struggled to control my big emotions. I could barely sing; tears stung my eyes and emotion rose in my throat. Then the words of the hymn brought peace, and thoughts of dancing a waltz flitted through my mind and stayed throughout the service. As I prayed, I remembered God's promise to be with me, to lead and guide me and my son.

The day before Jacob was to leave for college, my husband got sick and couldn't make the drive. By the end of that day, I also became ill with body aches and a fever. So instead of taking our son to college, we got COVID tests. Thankfully, we all tested negative. Eventually, my husband and I drove Jacob to school—four days after he was supposed to arrive. He missed all the fun gatherings before the semester started. When we moved him in, most of the residents on his floor were at dinner, sports practice, or off with newly formed friends.

Leaving my firstborn alone in his dorm room and getting back into the car to begin our drive home broke my heart. Friends had told me not to look in the rearview mirror as we left. I didn't listen. I looked back and saw Jacob standing there alone. I wanted to open the door and run back to Jacob and not go until I knew he would be okay.

The door stayed shut.

I sobbed. I didn't know how I could ever stop crying. During those moments, God reminded me through the promises in His Word: He would take the lead. He also reminded me He would be with Jacob and could help him in ways I could not.

EL SHADDAI REMEMBERS ISHMAEL

As we continue with our story in Genesis 17, Abraham's love for his oldest son tugs at my heartstrings.

READ GENESIS 17:18–22

Ishmael, Abraham's firstborn son, was thirteen years old by this time. As we read verse 18, we wonder what Abraham means when he says, "Oh that Ishmael might live before you!" Bible scholars have different ideas on what Abraham was thinking. Was Abraham asking God to please remember Ishmael with favor and bless him with eternal life? Maybe Abraham was simply praying that Ishmael would live a faithful and holy life. If God's response is an indication, Abraham may have again been offering a solution to the covenant because he doubts if Sarah can conceive. He may think, "Ishmael is my son, and Hagar belongs to Sarah; God could work through him to make the promises come true."

I love God's response here. First, He lets Abraham know that he will have a son with Sarah; Isaac will be the child of the promise. Then God says, "As for Ishmael, I have heard you; behold, I have blessed him and will make him fruitful and multiply him greatly. He shall father twelve princes, and I will make him into a great nation" (Genesis 17:20).

Consider these points:

- Ishmael's name means "God hears you."
- God made Ishmael a great nation. He was the father of the Arabian tribes.
- While Ishmael was not the son of the covenant, he received the promise of the covenant.

What surprises you about this story?

Discussion Question 34: How do you see God's grace poured out in the lives of Abraham, Sarah, and Ishmael? Where do you see God's grace for you in your life?

Isaac was born when Abraham was one hundred years old and Sarah was ninety. El Shaddai kept His promise.

The patriarchs knew God as El Shaddai. We see this name woven throughout the stories of Abraham, Isaac, and Jacob spanning Genesis 18–50. It would be a challenge to try to cover it all here, so I encourage you to read the rest of Genesis and watch their stories unfold.

Discussion Question 35: How does knowing God as El Shaddai—the sufficient one—change how you view your daily life?

Reflect on God's timing in your life and how it has drawn you into a place of deeper trust in Him.

Day 4: Rescued from Bitterness

> Let all bitterness and wrath and anger and clamor and slander be put away from you, along with all malice. Be kind to one another, tenderhearted, forgiving one another, as God in Christ forgave you. (Ephesians 4:31–32)

Have you ever been stuck in a pit of bitterness, mired in wretched words or actions taken against you? Reflect on that now.

Bitterness squeezes out the fruit of the spirit (love, joy, peace, patience, kindness, goodness, faithfulness, gentleness, and self-control; see Galatians 5:22–23) from your heart and leaves behind a rotten crop of unforgiveness.

I never intend for bitterness to be my destination, but sometimes I still end up there. For me, it starts when I focus on the ways people have done me wrong. I think I am merely venting, but soon I lose control. My complaints are a flashing neon sign pointing out all offenses done to me. I think that healing will come if I just get these offenses off my chest. I feel justified in my anger to see the expression on a listener's face when I explain the challenges I've experienced. In those moments, I enjoy the feelings that bitterness stirs up in me: vindication, justification, and pride. But telling my stories to get sympathy in return never gets rid of bitterness. It doesn't go away; rather, it settles deep and grows roots. Instead of healing, it destroys.

Discussion Question 36: Have you ever been bitter? What caused it? How did you deal with it?

We can learn a lot from the story of Joseph about bitterness and what it can do to you and your family.

READ GENESIS 37

Jacob had twelve sons, but his favorite was Joseph, and everyone knew it. The older sons felt the sting of knowing their baby brother held a treasured place in their father's heart they would never fill. Their bitterness toward Joseph grew and grew.

God gave Joseph the gift of interpreting dreams. We know why it was crucial for Joseph to have this ability, but his brothers didn't. They knew only that the favored son talked about his dreams and told them that someday they would bow down before him. If Joseph were my younger brother, I would probably be annoyed too.

Jacob gave Joseph a beautiful tunic, and he wore it in front of his brothers. Scripture isn't clear if Joseph knew how much his brothers disliked him. But because he showed off his tunic in front of his brothers, one would think either he was flaunting it or he didn't have a clue.

The brothers plotted to kill him, but Reuben intervened and said, "Let's just throw him in a pit and tell our father the wild animals got him." He planned to come back to save Joseph and bring him home to their father, but the other brothers saw some Ishmaelite traders and sold Joseph to them. The brothers then headed home with the torn tunic to tell Jacob their brother was dead.

Joseph could have jumped into the same pit of bitterness his brothers were in, but he didn't. Repeatedly, we read how God was with Joseph and helped him overcome every challenge. He was thrown into jail because of a lie told by Potiphar's wife, but God used even that for good: in prison, Joseph's divine gift of dream interpretation was revealed. Eventually, Joseph was released under the care of Pharaoh and rose to be second-in-command of all Egypt.

When Joseph saw his brothers, who had come to Egypt to beg for food, he could have killed them and no one would have stopped him. But he didn't. Joseph did not hold his brothers' sins against them; instead, he invited them to live in Egypt and be provided for.

I've always paused at what Joseph said to his brothers. I've come back to his response many times when I am struggling to forgive someone. Joseph told his brothers that what they intended for evil, God used for good to help save His people from starvation. Joseph saw God's hand in all of it. Joseph's response reminds me of Romans 8:28: "And we know that for those who love God all things work together for good, for those who are called according to His purpose." Sometimes we will not see the good that God is working out for us, and in those moments, we can ask God to strengthen our faith and give us His peace.

God didn't leave Joseph in his greatest time of need, and He won't leave you either. El Shaddai worked behind the scenes to make sure Joseph received the position that he did. As you think about how Joseph rose in his position, meditate on how only God could have orchestrated his life. And as you have time, read all of Genesis 45 and consider what it must have been like for Joseph and his brothers to face one another.

This story holds so many layers of forgiveness. Not only do we see reconciliation between Joseph and his brothers, but we also see Jacob forgiving his sons for their deception and the evilness of their plan.

I can only imagine the scene between Jacob and Joseph when they saw each other again. They must have experienced a mixture of joy and sorrow over all the time they had missed. Through it all, Jacob and Joseph did not let bitterness grow in their hearts. They trusted in El Shaddai to help them forgive and move past the hurt. And He will do the same for us.

Family drama is a part of life. We are a collection of broken sinners trying to relate to one another in a broken, messed-up world.

Forgiveness is hard.

I learned a lot about forgiveness from my grandma Katherine. I was fuzzy on the details, but my grandparents had divorced when it was still an uncommon thing to do. When I was little, I was aware that my grandpa was an alcoholic. As I got older, I learned my grandpa left my grandma for another woman. Grandpa left his family in poverty. My mom told us stories about how financially unsettled life was for her growing up. In the winter, she and her brother gathered cardboard boxes to burn in their wood stove to help make the woodpile last longer. My grandpa could have given money to help, but he chose to let them live destitute.

Nevertheless, Grandma was always kind to Grandpa at family gatherings at which both of them were present. The more I learned about them, the more I wondered how she could show kindness to someone who had caused so much pain for her and her children. I asked how she was able to be kind to him. She said, "Bitterness and hatred will destroy you. It's better to let go of your anger and give it to God."

Eventually, my grandfather received treatment for his alcoholism, and I have fond memories of fishing trips and time spent with him. Unfortunately, while I was in college, he slipped back into alcoholism, and more heartache followed. My relationship with my grandfather was filled with ups and downs, and my grandmother always encouraged me to forgive him. But it was hard.

One night, many years later, the phone rang. It was Grandpa. He apologized for the hurt he had caused over the years. He was broken and remorseful. I told him that night that I had forgiven him, but it was a process to work through the emotional layers caused from grieving all that had been lost and all that never was.

The more you love someone, the greater the pain you feel if the relationship breaks. Yet I know that someday in heaven, I will enjoy a restored relationship with my grandpa. If there is fishing in heaven, he will know the best spots.

Forgiveness in families and friendships can be difficult. El Shaddai, our all-sufficient God, gives us grace and strength needed to forgive.

I've learned the following truths about forgiveness. I pray they can help you too:

- We forgive because Jesus forgave us first.
- Forgiveness is only possible because our Savior died on the cross for us.
- When you forgive someone, you are not condoning their offense; you are releasing the situation to God.

- Forgiveness is an act of your will. If you wait until you feel like it, when your emotions settle down, or when you aren't hurt, you won't do it.
- You can forgive someone and still feel the hurt of betrayal. That doesn't mean you haven't forgiven them.
- Forgiveness is a process.
- Your unwillingness to forgive someone ends up hurting you more than the other person. God commands us to forgive.
- God's grace is enough to help you forgive.
- Setting boundaries in relationships, especially difficult ones, is good and healthy.
- Don't let bitterness destroy your soul.
- Repentance is a part of forgiveness, whether you are repenting of holding onto unforgiveness or because you have sinned against someone.

Do you have a relationship with which you struggle? Is there someone who has hurt you deeply and you cannot let it go? Write about it now.

Maybe you have a recurring or unresolved disagreement with your spouse, sibling, parent, in-law, or child. Take some time to think about that relationship and remember that El Shaddai will give you the strength to forgive through His Word and the Lord's Supper. He knows your hurt and pain. He knows all the ugly details, even those you cannot share with your best friends because it's too painful. Pour out your heart to El Shaddai and ask Him to help you forgive. Depending on the situation, this process might take a while to work through. There is no shame in seeking out a Christian counselor or asking your pastor for help.

Discussion Question 37: How have you struggled with forgiveness? How can knowing God as El Shaddai help you?

El Shaddai knows your heart, and He wants to help you. If you are struggling to forgive someone in your life, take some time now to bring the situation to Him in prayer.

Day 5: Grace Received Is Powerful

READ MATTHEW 14

Peter sat in the boat, exhausted from fighting the wind and the waves. It had been a long day, and the disciples wanted to get away for a while to mourn the loss of their friend John the Baptist.

The crowds had followed them though, and Jesus had had compassion on them. He spent time talking with them, preaching to them, and healing them. After several hours, the people were hungry, so Jesus had miraculously multiplied a boy's meal of fish and bread to feed more than five thousand people, with plenty of food left over.

Jesus, the man, needed time by Himself to talk to His Father in heaven, and so He sent the disciples off in the boat to sail to the other side of the sea. But what should have taken only a few hours turned into an all-night battle against the raging storm.

Then, in the early morning hours before sunrise, Jesus came out to them walking on water. The disciples cried out in fear, thinking He might be a ghost.

> But immediately Jesus spoke to them, saying, "Take heart; it is I. Do not be afraid." And Peter answered Him, "Lord, if it is You, command me to come to You on the water." He said, "Come." So Peter got out of the boat and walked on the water and came to Jesus. But when he saw the wind, he was afraid, and beginning to sink he cried out, "Lord, save me." (Matthew14:27–30)

When I served as a director of Christian education, I was on the program planning team for one of our district youth gatherings. Along with my sister Jimella and another DCE, Jeff, our job was to pick a theme for the gathering. We chose "Get a Grip." *Grip* was an acronym:

Grace

Received

Is

Powerful

Peter was a man of the sea, and he knew his place was in the boat, yet in a moment of faith, he stepped out of the boat to walk with Jesus. He didn't think it through; he just did it.

However, because Peter knew the sea, he focused on the waves crashing around him, and fear took over. The sea began to pull him under. Peter knew he was in trouble, and he cried out to the only One who could save him.

Imagine the hand of Jesus reaching into the water to grasp (or grip) Peter's hand. Peter received grace as Jesus pulled him up out of the water and into the boat. As they climbed into the boat, the wind and the waves stilled. The disciples worshiped Jesus and said, "Truly You are the Son of God" (v. 32).

Jesus extends the same salvation to us when He reaches down to pull us up from the storms of our sin. We cannot save ourselves; only He can, through His grace. The grace we receive from Jesus is powerful and changes our lives forever.

JESUS CHOSE PETER

I love studying the life of Peter.

Peter was a close friend of Jesus. He had traveled with Jesus and heard His lessons firsthand. He had witnessed Jesus' miracles and had himself been pulled from certain death by Jesus' gracious hand. But fear caused him to forget everything Jesus taught him. When Jesus told Peter he would deny Him three times, Peter swore he would never do that. And yet, before the night was over, Peter was weeping tears of bitterness because he had, in fact, denied Jesus.

Because of fear and shame, Peter hid while Jesus died on the cross. He must have been tortured with thoughts that Jesus was gone forever. Then, the joy Peter felt on Easter morning when he discovered Jesus was alive must have mingled with uncertainty of how Jesus might treat him. Would Jesus ever trust him again to be one of His disciples and one of His close friends?

He would. At the end of the Book of John, we watch Jesus forgive Peter and place the Church in his care (John 21:15–19).

As you think about the life of Peter and read his words in 1 Peter 1:2, "May grace and peace be multiplied to you," what images of Jesus do you think flashed through his mind?

Discussion Question 38: Where in your life could you use grace and peace multiplied right now?

Where have you seen grace and peace multiplied in your life in the past?

I love learning about Peter because I see myself in his behavior. I see God's grace and peace multiplied to me through the daily gift of love from my husband. I have a lot of health issues, and our daily life is tested because of it. Troy never complains; he loves me through all the challenges.

My compromised health often leaves me feeling anxious and helpless, and my faith wavers. Still, El Shaddai meets me right in the middle of my thoughts and breathes His peace over me. He gives me strength on the days when I can't muster my own. And I am learning to rest and trust in Him. I am often like Peter; I cry out, "Jesus, save me! I don't know what to do."

Paul, like Peter, received God's grace multiplied to him many times over. We, too, have received endless grace, through Jesus, our Savior.

Paul writes in 2 Corinthians 12:9:

> But He said to me, "My grace is sufficient for you, for My power is made perfect in weakness." Therefore I will boast all the more gladly of my weaknesses, so that the power of Christ may rest upon me.

Discussion Question 39: In what ways do you need to be reminded that El Shaddai's grace is sufficient for you? Where in your life can Jesus offer you rest?

Draw near to El Shaddai in His Word, and give thanks for His grace for where you are in your life right now.

Week 4 Group Study Questions

El Shaddai

El (God) Shaddai: *Sustainer, all-sufficient*

Pronunciation: *ĕl shad-dah'-ee*

El Shaddai is mentioned forty-eight times in the Bible; the Book of Job mentions El Shaddai thirty-one times alone. Job's story deals with heartbreaking loss. El Shaddai strengthened him with His sufficiency to continue. From his story, we see that God is present with us and that His peace cannot be taken away from us. Martin Luther said "this name indicates the might and power of God. . . . He alone . . . has power over everything, needs no one's help, and is able to give all things to all."

Bible Verse: *"He who dwells in the shelter of the Most High will abide in the shadow of the Almighty." (Psalm 91:1)*

REFLECTIONS

- What stories stood out to you the most from this week's sessions? Why?
- What did you learn about God as El Shaddai?
- Read Psalm 91. List the promises you see.

DISCUSSION QUESTIONS

30. What does *abide* mean to you?

31. How does knowing God as El Shaddai help you?

32. Do you remember your Baptism? Do you know your baptismal birthday? How has remembering your Baptism encouraged you?

33. How might remembering Abraham's story encourage your faith?

34. How do you see God's grace poured out in the lives of Abraham, Sarah, and Ishmael? Where do you see God's grace for you in your life?

35. How does knowing God as El Shaddai—the sufficient one—change how you view your daily life?

36. Have you ever been bitter? What caused it? How did you deal with it?

37. How have you struggled with forgiveness? How can knowing God as El Shaddai help you?

38. Where in your life could you use grace and peace multiplied right now?

39. In what ways do you need to be reminded that El Shaddai's grace is sufficient for you? Where in your life can Jesus offer you rest?

BENEDICTION

The LORD bless you and keep you;
The LORD make His face to shine upon you and be gracious to you;
The LORD lift up His countenance upon you and give you peace. (Numbers 6:24–26)

Jir'eh

Jir'eh: *Yahweh will see to it*

Pronunciation: *Ji-rah*

In Genesis 22:14, Abraham calls the place Jir'eh, which shows us who God is and what He does for us—God will provide, and He sees to our needs. This is a name of a place, and so when we learn that our God is a God who sees, we remember how God provided for Abraham and how He provides for us. Most important, God provided a sacrifice in place of our sins. That sacrifice—Jesus—is the fulfillment of God's promise to provide salvation for us.

Memory Verse: *" 'The L*ORD* is my portion,' says my soul, 'therefore I will hope in Him.' " (Lamentations 3:24)*

Day 1: Shattered Dreams Made New

The cruel words were like darts to my heart. "Miss Moorhead, how can you be so stupid?" My eyelids stung as if a thousand needles were poking them, but I managed to keep the tears inside. I would not cry in front of the worst kind of bully, my ninth-grade algebra teacher.

I felt sympathy fill the room from my silent classmates, who dared not look up lest he call upon them and subject them to the same humiliation.

Words failed to form on my lips. I wondered how to explain that I had spent five hours the night before on one problem and still didn't understand how to solve it. The teacher knew I shouldn't be in his classroom; it was too advanced for me, but he refused to let me transfer out. The school had made an error placing me in algebra I before I had taken pre-algebra. My mom had made countless phone calls and visits to the school, begging them to put me in another class, but no one listened.

Those heartless words haunted me throughout high school and were amplified several years later by the guidance counselor, who said, "Miss Moorhead, you are not college material. You will never make it in college." Those words crushed my confidence.

The Bible says, "The Lord is near to the brokenhearted and saves the crushed in spirit" (Psalm 34:18). God was near during those long high school years as I struggled with feelings of inadequacy. My parents and siblings were supportive and loving. Our church youth group provided a space for me to grow and develop leadership skills. I loved my church family and the time I spent learning and serving with them. And not all of the faculty and staff at my high school were so harsh. A couple of teachers encouraged me, which gave me confidence to be myself. They made a huge difference in my life, inspiring hope for my future.

Discussion Question 40: How has God provided for you when life is hard?

Fast-forward to my senior year. After weeks of talking to a recruiter for the Air Force, I began making plans for the physical entrance examination. One afternoon, I received a phone call from the recruiter to finalize some details. Among his questions, he asked if I had any lung ailments.

"Yes, actually. I have allergy-induced asthma."

Before he had time to say another word, I added, "But I barely use my inhaler!"

There was a long, painful silence on the other end. Finally, he sighed and said, "I am sorry, Michelle, but asthma disqualifies you from serving in the military."

My dreams shattered. I was a high school senior without plans.

Stupid.

Failure.

Not smart or healthy enough.

These words screeched through my mind. *See, they told you: you would never be enough.*

Of course, my story didn't end there. I didn't know it then, but something was about to happen that would change everything.

> The heart of man plans his way, but the LORD establishes his steps. (Proverbs 16:9)

After days of crying and wondering what I would do with my life, my dad told me I needed to stop crying, pull myself together, and hear him out.

His words were exactly what I needed to hear: "You've let people who do not know you form the thoughts you have about who you are and what you can and cannot do. Your mom and I believe in you, and we think you are smart enough to go to college. Have you thought that maybe God has different and better plans for you? He will provide everything you need to get through college, if that is where He is leading you."

I sat there. I knew he was right. I had forgotten I was a child of God. He would provide for me.

My first year of college, I attended our local community college. As I began down the path I never thought I would take, I was nervous. *What if I fail?* However, once I was in an encouraging academic environment, I discovered I was passionate about learning. I learned to study in a way that helped me learn and retain information. I even made the dean's list.

After a year at community college, I transferred to Concordia University in St. Paul, Minnesota. I loved everything about that college. As I began to get my bearings around campus and became involved with different groups, I met some students in the Director of Christian Education (DCE) program. I was intrigued when I found out the program prepared graduates to serve full-time in youth ministries, Christian education programs, and family ministries. I started to attend their Bible study sessions and asked a lot of questions. As my interest and enthusiasm grew, I frequently asked God if this was the vocation He was leading me to. It's clear to me now that Yahweh provided me with people to talk to who led me to serve as a DCE. God directed me away from military service and toward church work. He had been unfolding the details in ways I could not comprehend.

God unfolded details for Abram too, as we will see in this week's readings. God gave him faith to trust in His promises and to be confident in Him. And God kept His covenant with Abram, making him the father of a great nation that includes us and, most important, includes our Savior.

Life sometimes looks different than our plans. How can we move forward when we feel unsure about the future? We can look to God's Word and His promises to us and find rest in Him.

READ JOHN 15:4–11

Notice what Jesus tells us:

- *Abide* means "to remain." Jesus will remain by your side through all things.
- Jesus is the vine, and He provides what is needed for the branches.
- Jesus invites us to abide in His love.

- Jesus gives us His joy.

Joy is not the absence of sorrow; it is knowing Jesus our Savior is with us in all things. We don't need to worry about what will come next or sort out all of the details; we can move forward, trusting the promises of Jesus. We rest in who He is and who we are in Him.

How does your life look different from what you planned? How has God helped you?

SCRIPTURE PRAYER

But this I call to mind, and therefore I have hope: The steadfast love of the LORD never ceases; His mercies never come to an end; they are new every morning; great is Your faithfulness. "The LORD is my portion," says my soul, "therefore I will hope in Him." (Lamentations 3:21–24)

BENEDICTION

The LORD bless you and keep you;
The LORD make His face to shine upon you and be gracious to you;
The LORD lift up His countenance upon you and give you peace. (Numbers 6:24–26)

As you enter this week, be in the presence of the One who knows your needs and provides for them. He loves you beyond measure. Remember the gifts God has given to you through the Divine Service. He has removed your sins from you; He has strengthened your faith through the hearing of the Word and through receiving the Sacrament. Abide in His promises to you, and rest in His faithfulness toward you.

Day 2: Abraham Walks in Faith

Now faith is the assurance of things hoped for, the conviction of things not seen. (Hebrews 11:1)

After the flood, after the people had again turned away from God and built the tower of Babel, God chose Abram as the father of His people. In Genesis 12, we read that God called Abram, a descendant of Noah's son Shem and an idolater, to leave his country and travel to a place God would show him. The Lord promised to bless Abram and Sarai, to make his name great, and to bless all the families of the earth through Abram's offspring. Abram, who was seventy-five years old and childless, believed God and obeyed His calling. He and his wife, Sarai, traveled to Egypt and eventually settled in Canaan—where they set up their tent and waited. After ten years, a frustrated Sarai convinced Abram to beget that son through her servant Hagar. Ishmael was born. Ishmael, however, was not the son God had promised, so Abram and Sarai had to wait another thirteen years for the promised son, Isaac. But having to wait twenty-five years for their son was not the most difficult thing Abram (now renamed Abraham) was called to do.

The account in Genesis 22 shows us that when Abraham heard the word from the Lord to go and do what He commanded, he obeyed because he had received faith to trust God's promises. He also was tested beyond anything we are likely to endure. God told Abraham:

> Take your son, your only son Isaac, whom you love, and go
> to the land of Moriah, and offer him there as a burnt offering
> on one of the mountains of which I shall tell you. (Genesis
> 22:2)

It was a three-day journey to Moriah, but Abraham didn't question God, stall for more time with Isaac, or say he couldn't leave his elderly wife. He got everything ready, and he went. Just as we read about his response to God in Genesis 12, here we read that Abraham heard the word from the Lord and received faith from God to go and do.

Abraham remembered the promises God had made to him, and he had faith that God would fulfill those promises. The writer of Hebrews says:

> By faith Abraham, when he was tested, offered up Isaac, and
> he who had received the promises was in the act of offering
> up his only son, of whom it was said, "Through Isaac shall
> your offspring be named." He considered that God was able
> even to raise him from the dead, from which, figuratively
> speaking, he did receive him back. (Hebrews 11:17–19)

Early the next morning, Abraham saddled his donkey and cut wood for the burnt offering. He gathered two servants to help him, and he made sure Isaac was ready to travel. He headed where God had commanded him to go.

After the third day, Abraham lifted his gaze and saw the place from a distance. He told the servants to stay with the donkey. "Isaac and I will worship over there and return to you" (see Genesis 22:5). Abraham gathered the supplies for the sacrifice and laid the wood across Isaac's shoulders. Isaac looked to Abraham and asked, "Where is the lamb for the sacrifice?" (see verse 7). Abraham told Isaac that God would provide the lamb for the offering.

Notice what this account shows us:

- Abraham told the servants they would come back. He didn't know how God would keep His promises to him, but he trusted God even when it didn't make sense.
- Abraham remembered that he and Sarah had conceived a child in their old age. God kept His promise.
- Abraham remembered that God included Ishmael in the covenant, even though Ishmael was not the son God had promised. God could have cast Ishmael aside, but He didn't.

- Abraham had faith that God would provide for them. The word *provide* in Hebrew means "to see to it."

When they arrived at the place to which God had directed them, Abraham built an altar. He laid the wood on the altar, bound his son, and placed him on the altar. Then he took his knife and raised it to sacrifice Isaac.

Can you imagine the scene? A father who had waited until the fullness of time for his beloved son to be born is getting ready to sacrifice him. (I once saw a dramatic reenactment of this story, and it was horrifying to see Abraham holding the knife over his son.) What kind of God would finally keep His promise to a very old man to provide a son for him and then ask that man to lay that son on an altar and kill him? Imagine the heartbreak and the agony Abraham must have felt! Still, Abraham's incredible faith in God kept him moving forward with what God had asked him to do.

We are not told what Isaac said or how he reacted to Abraham tying his hands and putting him on the altar. Because the Bible doesn't tell us otherwise, we guess Isaac was obedient to his father and trusted what God had commanded—just as Abraham was obedient to his Father and trusted His command. We do not know how old Isaac was when this took place, but some scholars believe he was a young man. If so, he could have overpowered Abraham if he had wanted to. But Isaac was obedient, even unto death if necessary.

But then the Angel of the Lord (Jesus) stopped Him. Jesus, the One who would become the final sacrifice for our sins, stopped Abraham.

> But the angel of the LORD called to him from heaven and said, "Abraham, Abraham!" And he said, "Here I am." He said, "Do not lay your hand on the boy or do anything to him, for now I know that you fear God, seeing you have not withheld your son, your only son, from Me." (Genesis 22:11–12)

How have you trusted God in an impossible situation?

> And Abraham lifted up his eyes and looked, and behold, behind him was a ram, caught in a thicket by his horns. And Abraham went and took the ram and offered it up as a burnt

offering instead of his son. So Abraham called the name of that place, "The LORD will provide"; as it is said to this day, "On the mount of the LORD it shall be provided." (Genesis 22:13–14)

Of course, this story foreshadows how God provided Jesus as the Lamb who bore our sins in His sacrificial death on the cross. The Lord provided for Abraham on Mount Moriah by providing a ram for the sacrifice. God continued to provide for His people by having King Solomon build the temple on Mount Moriah. Through sacrifices at that temple, God provided atonement for His people's sins; however, these sacrifices weren't permanent. They were offered over and over again. In His timing, God provided the final sacrifice through His Son, Jesus, on Golgotha, which is considered a part of Mount Moriah.

The Lord continued to meet the needs of His people:

And the angel of the LORD called to Abraham a second time from heaven and said, "By Myself I have sworn, declares the LORD, because you have done this and have not withheld your son, your only son, I will surely bless you, and I will surely multiply your offspring as the stars of heaven and as the sand that is on the seashore. And your offspring shall possess the gate of his enemies, and in your offspring shall all the nations of the earth be blessed, because you have obeyed My voice." (Genesis 22:15–18)

Obedient father Abraham received the covenant promise that through his offspring (his seed), the Messiah would come. That nation, made up of people as countless as the stars and the grains of sand on the seashore, is blessed through the Messiah.

Discussion Question 41: What questions would you have for Abraham and Isaac if you could sit with them and talk to them about this story?

Walk in faith that God continuously provides for you, especially in the atoning sacrifice of His Son, Jesus. Reflect on a time that you have seen God's faithful provision for you.

Day 3: God Will Provide

As we read yesterday, Genesis 22 shows us that by faith Abraham trusted God to keep His promises, even when they didn't make sense.

Sometimes we get nervous when we hear the word *faith*, because we think choosing and strengthening our faith is dependent upon our actions. But faith is a gift from God. We receive it from the Holy Spirit through the Word and Baptism. He strengthens our faith when we receive Holy Communion. Faith grows because God nourishes and sustains it.

Faith believes Yahweh provides for us and meets our needs, even when we cannot anticipate how things might work out. We trust in the promises of the One who will never break His promises to us, because we have examples of His faithfulness in the Bible and in our own lives. God doesn't fail us.

In this week's sessions, we look at accounts in the Bible and real-life stories of people who had faith in God's promises. One of these people was Moses.

> By faith Moses, when he was born, was hidden for three
> months by his parents, because they saw that the child
> was beautiful, and they were not afraid of the king's edict.
> (Hebrews 11:23)

I remember hearing this lesson in Sunday School as a little girl. We would see pictures of baby Moses floating in a basket in the river, then we'd see a picture of an Egyptian princess scooping him up from the basket. I was so familiar with the story as a child that I can still recite it, but it didn't impact me until I became a mom.

READ EXODUS 2:1–10

The first time I left my first child at home with my husband, although it was for only a couple of hours, anxious thoughts made my new-mom mind race with all the possibilities of what could go wrong. I could not relax at all.

That's why I can't imagine the anguish Jochebed must have felt when she placed her baby in a basket to float down the Nile River among the crocodiles and cobras. But she didn't have a choice.

The Egyptian pharaoh was afraid the Hebrew slaves would become too populous and too powerful for him to control, so he ordered all newborn Hebrew boys to be thrown into the Nile and drowned. Jochebed had managed to keep her infant son hidden for a while, but there is no way to keep a three-month-old baby quiet and hidden indefinitely. She did what she had to do.

In my imagination, she placed her baby in the basket, covered him up, and kissed his cheek. She looked upon his precious face, memorizing every detail, and inhaled his baby scent one last time. As she placed him in the Nile, she entrusted him to God's care. She put her broken heart into God's hands too, looking to Him for solace. Jochebed had to hold in her grief because she didn't want to draw attention to the water's edge and risk the pharaoh's soldiers finding baby Moses floating among the reeds.

Discussion Question 42: What are your favorite details from this story of how God provided for Jochebed and Moses?

The Lord provided for her baby beyond anything she could have prayed for. She set him afloat not knowing if she would ever see him again. God had plans for Moses, so He made a way for him to be preserved—by the daughter of his enemy, no less! Jochebed's daughter, Miriam, was in the right place at the right time to suggest how Pharaoh's daughter might handle the foundling. His own mother became his wet nurse, and she was able to teach and take care for him for three more years, until he came under the protection of the princess.

What do you need to let go of in your life and hand over into God's care?

TRUSTING GOD WHEN IT DOESN'T MAKE SENSE

My parents are the most excellent teachers of the faith I've ever had. They don't just tell me to trust God; they also show what it looks like to trust Him in all situations. The following example from my college experience illustrates their faith in God's provision.

My twin sister and I attended the same college and majored in the same program. I'll never forget the day we discovered we would both need cars to drive to our internships. We had heard rumors that DCE program participants would need a car, but we didn't look into it. It was impossible for our family to provide two extra cars for us, so I guess we just put it out of our minds for as long as we could.

One day, our professor mentioned in class that our year-long internships might be anywhere in the United States, and we wouldn't live on campus. We would need daily transportation—a car. Jimella and I glanced at each other and looked away quickly. There was no money for one car, let alone two. It was all our parents could do to help with our college expenses. We would have to tell them about needing cars, but the dread I felt about having this conversation choked me up. There was no extra money, and telling our parents about a need they couldn't meet made me sad and fearful. I was reluctant to be the cause of their emotional burden of guilt, but I had to. So, with a trembling voice, I told Mom and Dad we would both need cars to complete our internships to become directors of Christian education.

The phone line went silent. Jimella and I leaned in close to hear what they had to say. We each held our breath and prayed Mom and Dad would not tell us to change our majors. Dad's voice broke the silence loud and clear: "I believe God led both of you to this, and I believe He will provide. God has taken care of us all these years, and He won't stop now. You both focus on school, and your mom and I will pray about it and see what God has in store."

So we waited, studied, and prayed for a miracle. And we got one.

One day, my dad received unexpected back pay from his employer.

Our parents went to a dealership to pick out two used cars. When they paid for the vehicles, the price was the exact amount as the check from Dad's employer.

Was this a coincidence? I don't think so. Yahweh, our Provider, saw to it. He provided right down to the penny. My parents, sister, and I trusted God to hear our prayers and respond according to His will for us. Because God called us into ministry, God provided the means for us to be equipped to serve Him. If our ministry was not God's will, then He wouldn't have provided a way.

The day I received my college diploma, I choked back tears and gave thanks to God. He had provided for every need and beyond. Over the years, people have asked if I sent my diploma to the high school guidance counselor and teacher who were so critical of me. I chuckle and shake my head.

I didn't need to prove myself to those who didn't know me. I had all I needed in the One who knew me best. God always has the final say over who you are. In Him, you are enough, because He is enough.

I REMEMBER; I REMEMBER NOT

If you are like me, sometimes you need help remembering you can trust God. We don't mean to forget, but we see our problems through the lens of our finite abilities instead of remembering that our God is infinite.

During the beginning of the COVID pandemic, I participated in an online retreat called "Trusting God," led by Jan Johnson and Matt Rhodes. Throughout the retreat, they gave encouragement and simple practices to help us remember we can trust God. These two simple practices they shared have helped me:

- When someone asks how you are doing amid a difficult circumstance, respond with "I am trusting God." Saying those words reminds us that we can, indeed, trust God in all things. It puts the focus on God and not the circumstance.
- When you face uncertainty and wonder how you will make it through, tell yourself you can trust God for the next ten minutes.

Repeat this as often as you need to.[11]

These practices have helped me to shift my thinking from the problem to the One (Jesus) who can help me get through whatever I am facing.

You can trust Him to see you through your days, dear friend.

Reflect on God's faithfulness to you in your life.

Day 4: Held by God

In 1993, long before the internet and cell phones, my younger sister, Sheila, traveled to Moscow, Russia, to be a missionary. I will never forget saying goodbye to her at the airport and realizing it would be almost a year before we would see her again.

Sheila was calm and cool, and I was the exact opposite. Fear twisted inside me, and I could barely talk as I tried to say goodbye to her. I sobbed, and red blotches covered my face. I was a mess. She was the one traveling to the other side of the world, and she didn't even seem nervous. She said, "Michelle, why are you crying so much?"

I poured out my secret fears. Communism had fallen; as the country struggled to find order, the presence of organized crime had grown, and with it came unknown danger. "What if you die over there?" I blurted out.

Sheila looked at me and said, "Whether I live or die, I am with the Lord—what more could you ask for?" I knew she was right, and I remembered the little pin that I was about to give her as a farewell gift. It was in the shape of a hand—symbolizing God's hand—with the figure of a girl resting in the palm. I had purchased pins for Sheila, Jimella, our mom, and me to wear while Sheila was in Russia. The image was inspired by Isaiah 49:

> Can a woman forget her nursing child, that she should have
> no compassion on the son of her womb? Even these may
> forget, yet I will not forget you. Behold, I have engraved you
> on the palms of My hands; your walls are continually before
> Me. (vv. 15–16)

The time had come for our final hug, and with tears streaming down my cheeks and dripping off the end of my nose, I released her. My heart ached for the distance and the time we would be separated. But I was also excited for Sheila and all the people I knew she would touch with God's love. And I began to feel the peace that flows from faith in God's power. Sheila served as a missionary in Russia for two years. She was able to come home for about six weeks on furlough during that time. Otherwise, our family communicated by writing letters and a rare phone call, as overseas rates were expensive.

At the beginning of October 1993, Sheila called home to talk to our mom and let her know she was doing okay and was living with a Russian family. She said maybe we would see her on the news that night, because she had been in the vicinity of a political demonstration. Before Mom could get more information, including her phone number, they lost connection.

I had traveled to visit my parents that weekend, and we were keeping our eyes on the news from Moscow. The political unrest had reached a breaking point, and there was a battle over who would control their parliament. We watched the demonstrations and wondered how close Sheila was to the area. During that brief phone call, she talked about seeing people marching and all the major news networks that were there.

On October 4, Moscow was on the brink of a civil war. We watched in horror as military tanks rolled down the streets toward the parliament building and opened fire on it. The news reports compared it to the 1917 Bolshevik Revolution. We sat in shock and disbelief as we watched the events. Our Sheila was there, and we didn't know how to contact her. I prayed we wouldn't see her on television.

As the evening news ended, my parents' phone began to ring with calls from family and friends, asking if we had heard from Sheila. They all wanted to know the same thing. Was she safe?

Again and again, we repeated the message. "We don't know if she is okay. We can't contact her. Please pray for Sheila's safety and for the people of Russia."

Finally, the phone was quiet. I told my parents about the conversation I had with Sheila at the airport. I also gave Mom a figurine of the little girl carved in the palm of God's hand. We reminded each other that we could trust God to provide for her. And we took comfort knowing that Sheila was with a Russian family that treated her like a daughter and were very protective of her.

As my head nestled into my pillow, I prayed that God would continue to hold her in the palm of His hand. I awoke many times, and each time I did, I prayed for God to surround and enfold Sheila and my parents. It was a relief to put my faith in God's promises.

The following day the phone rang—it was Sheila! I'm not a track star, but I sprinted to the downstairs phone so Mom could be on the extension upstairs. We were overjoyed to hear her voice. She said she knew we would be worried by how the news media were portraying events taking place in Moscow. She told us it was terrible, but not as bad as the news was making it out to be. She assured us her Russian family was helping to keep her safe. They had forbidden her to go out until it was once again safe on the streets of Moscow.

READ JOHN 10:28–30

Whether our loved ones are within our embrace or beyond our reach and sight half the world away, we can be confident that God always holds His beloved children in His capable hands.

Sheila got very ill when she was there and had a reaction to a medication. Her Russian mother slept on the floor in her bedroom to make sure she could hear Sheila breathing through the night. We had no idea she was even sick until she wrote about it in one of her letters. Yahweh attended to Sheila's needs and provided for her in ways we could not.

In the years since Sheila's missionary service in Moscow, communication technology has expanded. Now, the internet, smartphones, email, video chat, and tracking apps connect us with our loved ones, and we've become obsessed with always knowing where they are and when they've read our messages. I used to think I would have more peace constantly knowing my loved ones are okay. Instead, I've noticed how much I rely on the apps, and I drive myself crazy with worry.

But worry, when it becomes our focus, is a lack of faith. Our God is powerful enough to part seas and still storms. He has protected His children in fiery furnaces, in lions' dens, and in battles. God does not intend for us to go blindly into dangerous situations, but He does equip us to go about the work He has set before us in our earthly vocations. God called Sheila to mission work in Moscow during a turbulent time in that city's history. She was faithful to the call and drew peace from knowing how God had preserved Jonah, for example, as well as the faithful missionaries who had served before her. He protected her and provided for her every second.

Our heavenly Father, who provides for the smallest sparrow in the sky, provides for your loved ones too. Each time we pray, "Thy will be done," we ask for His protection and provision and state our faith that He will keep His promises to provide it.

READ MATTHEW 6:25—34

Jesus tells us not to be anxious about our lives, because we cannot fix anything by worrying about it. We know that our Lord cares for the sparrow and cares even more for our loved ones, whether they are close beside us or far away. The Creator will provide for them and keep them in His care.

Discussion Question 43: How do you handle being apart from your loved ones?

If you tend to worry, what are some things you could do to help you remember to trust God?

In your journal time today, surrender your fears and worries, and trust God to provide for your loved ones wherever they are.

DAY 5: EXTRAVAGANT LOVE

READ LUKE 7:36–50

Simon, one of the Pharisees, invited Jesus to come for dinner. At feasts such as this one, people would come in and watch the hosts and guests eat. The poor would hope for scraps from the table.

It was customary at that time for dining tables to be low to the ground. Guests would sit on the floor or recline on low couches next to the table, either leaning on their left elbow with their legs and feet tucked away from the table or on their stomachs facing the table with their legs behind them. Anyone entering the room would not have been noticed right away. Luke 7:36 tells us that Jesus "reclined at table," so He was in this posture and was looking toward the other guests.

The woman would have approached Him from behind. We are not told how she knew Jesus, but it is clear she knew who He was, and she understood the love and forgiveness He could extend to her.

Luke doesn't tell us her name but refers to her as "a woman of the city, who was a sinner," from which we conclude she is a prostitute.

The woman stood behind Jesus. Overwhelmed by His grace, she wept, and her tears fell and covered His feet. Then she did the unthinkable: she bent low, unbound her hair, and wiped His feet with it. Women did not unbind their hair in public; that would have been scandalous. Then she poured out an expensive perfume—worth at least a year's wages—on Jesus' feet and wiped them dry with her hair.

Why would Jesus let a prostitute touch and kiss His feet? The others present were probably surprised that He didn't recoil and send her away. In fact, in the Jewish culture of Jesus' day, women were kept separate from men in public and in private.

Regardless, the woman worshiped Jesus at His feet. From her eyes flowed the sorrow of her sins. From her heart flowed love and adoration for Him who knew her name, sins, and her past and who offered her love, grace, and forgiveness.

I love this exchange between Jesus and Simon, especially since Simon didn't speak his reaction aloud—Jesus, God the Son, knew his thoughts.

> Now when the Pharisee who had invited Him saw this, he said to himself, "If this man were a prophet, He would have known who and what sort of woman this is who is touching Him, for she is a sinner." And Jesus answering said to him, "Simon, I have something to say to you." And he answered, "Say it, Teacher." "A certain moneylender had two debtors. One owed five hundred denarii, and the other fifty. When they could not pay, he cancelled the debt of both. Now which of them will love him more?" Simon answered, "The one, I suppose, for whom he cancelled the larger debt." And He said to him, "You have judged rightly." Then turning toward the woman He said to Simon, "Do you see this woman? I entered your house; you gave Me no water for My feet, but she has wet My feet with her tears and wiped them with her hair. You gave Me no kiss, but from the time I came in she has not ceased to kiss My feet. You did not anoint My head with oil, but she has anointed My feet with ointment. Therefore I tell you, her sins, which are many, are forgiven—for she loved much. But he who is forgiven little, loves little." (Luke 7:39–47)

Jesus exposed the Pharisee as a hypocrite. Let's give this account some context. In the preceding chapter, Jesus had been teaching the people about the kingdom of God. Earlier in chapter 7, Jesus had healed the centurion's servant and had raised the widow's son from the dead. And just before this meal at Simon's house, Jesus had confirmed that He was indeed the Messiah John the Baptist had prophesied about. Simon's dinner invitation wasn't a gesture of goodwill—it was an attempt to entrap Jesus, to expose

Him as a sham. Simon not only failed in his responsibility as host, but he also failed to prove that Jesus was a fraud.

The Pharisees, because of their elevated status in the community and knowledge of Scripture, did not view themselves as having much sin. They felt superior to everyone—including Jesus. They believed themselves to be holy because of their good works, and they would never have humbled themselves as the repentant prostitute did. So they did not understand the forgiveness Jesus offered her.

The woman was not forgiven because of her humility or her generous gift to Jesus or even her worship. She didn't earn forgiveness from Jesus; she received it freely, as a gift.

In my imagination, Jesus is still reclining at the table, and His host, Simon, is at the head of the same table. Jesus knows Simon's thoughts and responds with a lesson about the moneylender, which would resonate with a rich man like Simon. Then Jesus makes His point. The sinful woman, for whom it was not acceptable to be in the same room, was forgiven. She was forgiven because of her faith in Jesus. She was forgiven because she truly understood His grace.

Notice how Jesus treated the woman. He didn't pull away from her. If you were in the room watching this scene unfold, how do you think Jesus looked at her? I imagine His eyes were filled with compassion toward her, showing her unending love and grace.

Discussion Question 44: If you could sit with Jesus face-to-face to confess your sins, how do you think He would look at you? Take some time to think about this.

Here is the truth: Jesus looks at you with compassion and love. His love for you is more significant than your sin. Friend, sin seeks to separate you from God. Satan wants you to hang onto your shame and guilt. The devil dances with glee when you question your worth and wonder if you are enough—if you are worthy to step into the presence of God.

Jesus has proclaimed over you in the waters of your Baptism that you are enough. You do not need to carry the shame of your sin any longer, because He took all of it onto Himself on the cross and removed it from you. Jesus poured out His blood for us on the cross of Calvary. His blood given for us is more precious than gold or silver. The Lord provided the Lamb for the sacrifice. He saw to it that His grace covered us through the blood of His only Son, Jesus. You have been washed clean through the waters of Holy Baptism. You are only baptized once, but your Baptism is renewed daily by the power of the Holy Spirit.

I love the hymn "Chief of Sinners Though I Be." Consider the first two verses:

> Chief of sinners though I be,
> Jesus shed His blood for me,
> Died that I might live on high,
> Lives that I might never die.
> As the branch is to the vine,
> I am His, and He is mine.

> Oh, the height of Jesus' love,
> Higher than the heav'ns above,
> Deeper than the depths of sea,
> Lasting as eternity!
> Love that found me—wondrous thought!
> Found me when I sought Him not.[12]

Rest in these promises from the One who provides. He has ensured that your sins are removed, and He forgives you. He has provided a way for you to sit in the peace of His presence. Rest in His love and grace for you.

> For we do not have a high priest who is unable to sympathize with our weaknesses, but one who in every respect has been tempted as we are, yet without sin. Let us then with confidence draw near to the throne of grace, that we may receive mercy and find grace to help in time of need. (Hebrews 4:15–16)

Discussion Question 45: Once you have confessed your sins to God, what do you do? Do you hold onto them and try to fix them? How does that make you feel?

God's Law (the Commandments) show us our sin. None of us can keep His Law; therefore, each of us is condemned under His Law. In your journal time today, praise Him for providing us with a Redeemer!

WEEK 5 GROUP STUDY QUESTIONS

JIR'EH

Jir'eh: *Yahweh will provide; the Lord will see to it*

Pronunciation: *Ji-rah*

In Genesis 22:14, Abraham calls the place Jir'eh, which shows us who God is and what He does for us—God will provide, and He sees to our needs. This is a name of a place, and so when we learn that our God is a God who sees, we remember how God provided for Abraham and how He provides for us. Most important, God provided a sacrifice in place of our sins. That sacrifice—Jesus—is the fulfillment of God's promise to provide salvation for us.

Memory Verse: *"'The LORD is my portion,' says my soul, 'therefore I will hope in Him.'" (Lamentations 3:24)*

REFLECTIONS

- What stories stood out to you the most from this week's sessions? Why?
- What did you learn about God as Jir'eh?

DISCUSSION QUESTIONS

40. How has God provided for you when life is hard?

41. What questions would you have for Abraham and Isaac if you could sit with them and talk to them about this story?

42. What are your favorite details from this story of how God provided for Jochebed and Moses?

43. How do you handle being apart from your loved ones?

44. If you could sit with Jesus face-to-face to confess your sins, how do you think He would look at you? Take some time to think about this.

45. Once you have confessed your sins to God, what do you do? Do you hold onto them and try to fix them? How does that make you feel?

BENEDICTION

The LORD bless you and keep you;
The LORD make His face to shine upon you and be gracious to you;
The LORD lift up His countenance upon you and give you peace. (Numbers 6:24–26)

Shalom

Shalom: *God is peace (the name of the altar Gideon built)*

Pronunciation: *Shaw-lome'*

Used first by Gideon in Judges 6:24, Shalom describes the peace, completeness, harmony, and absence of conflict found only in God. Having asked for signs from God, and receiving them, Gideon was visited by an angel who spoke as the Lord Himself. Only Moses and Abraham had had such visitations. Bolstered in his faith, Gideon recognized that the Lord had been with the Israelites all along. So he built an altar at Ophrah, naming it "Shalom" as a reminder of God's presence, protection, and provision. When we learn that the Lord is Shalom, we remember that our peace is from Him alone.

Bible Verse: *"And the peace of God, which surpasses all understanding, will guard your hearts and your minds in Christ Jesus." (Philippians 4:7)*

Day 1: God's Peace Settles Your Heart

The paper crinkled under me as I sat on the cold exam table at the doctor's office. The ticking of the clock echoed through the room as my thoughts collided in a tangle of confusion. I couldn't begin to sort out my emotions.

The word *cancer* has a way of making the world stop. I obsessed over the word, desperate to know how my life might change if they confirmed it was in my body. There was a mass the size of a baseball on my ovary. From the X-rays, my doctor said he could not be certain if it was cancer, but since the mass was growing at a rapid rate, surgery would be needed within the week.

The doctor knew I longed to have another child, but he cautioned that if the mass were ovarian cancer, I would need a complete hysterectomy to give me the best chance at survival.

My life turned upside down, and I drove home in a fog. I only knew I wanted to see Troy. Thankfully, when I got home, our son, who wasn't yet two, was napping. My precious boy didn't see his mommy fall apart in his daddy's arms. As much as I wanted more children, I needed to be a mom to the one I had.

Thoughts poured forth from every corner of my soul.

What if I die?
Who will take care of Jacob?
What if he doesn't remember me?
What if Troy marries again?
Will he love her more than me?

My emotions were ugly, real, and raw. I couldn't process all the feelings, and I was appalled by my thoughts. Shame filled my heart until I brought all my concerns before God. Desperate for comfort, I sought my heavenly Father. His Word settled into my soul, and I was able to let go of worrying about the outcome. The Holy Spirit took my what-ifs and helped me focus on what is. The peace washing over me was unlike anything I've ever known. I was reminded that God loved Jacob and Troy more than I did and would take care of them no matter what. I held Jacob and watched him sleep. As I watched over my precious son, I knew that God was doing the same for all of us. My fear began to dissolve, and the comfort and confidence I have because of God's love for us brought peace. God poured out the gift of His peace and helped me to rest in His promises of forgiveness and eternal life with Him.

As the days went by and surgery loomed close, that peace remained. Questions drifted in and out of my mind, but I did not have the strength to sort through them. I knew Jesus, the source of peace, would take care of my needs, so I placed all my cares in His hands.

The day arrived. I hugged Jacob close, hoping and praying I would see those sweet blue eyes again and hear his little voice calling me *mommy*. As I passed my son into the arms of his father, I felt secure that he was also in the arms of the One who loves him more than anyone.

They prepped me for surgery, and through my tears, I said goodbye to Troy. Clinging to the promises of God, I waited for the procedure to begin. I was quiet. Noticing this, the doctor patted my arm.

"Michelle, are you all right?"

"Yes, I am just praying. When it is time to count backward, can I keep praying and talking to God instead?"

"Sure, Michelle. That sounds like a great plan."

I fell asleep with a peaceful heart, confident in my Savior's love. The next thing I knew, I was waking up and hearing the happy news.

"It isn't cancer. But," my doctor said, "you have a severe case of endometriosis. I know you are eager to have another child, so once you heal from surgery you can start trying. But I am concerned the scar tissue may keep you from becoming pregnant."

Each month we were hopeful, and each month we mourned. The anniversary of my surgery happened to coincide with Holy Week. After long conversations and prayer, Troy and I decided we would call an adoption agency the following week. Then, on Easter morning, we discovered to our great joy that we were pregnant. By Christmas, we held Matthew, whose name means "gift from God."

I still struggle with what-if thinking, and it keeps me from resting in the truth of God's Word. Do you struggle with this type of thinking too? Perhaps you are not teetering between life and death circumstances, but your situation is causing you to lose sleep. Maybe you overthink every conversation or you dwell on the worst that can happen.

I understand how thoughts can take over; I have struggled with this habit for years. But I have learned that God isn't mad about how we think. He knows our thoughts before we even consider them. And He loves us despite them. In fact, the Prince of Peace wants to meet us right where we are and help with our struggles.

> Rejoice in the Lord always; again I will say, rejoice. Let your reasonableness be known to everyone. The Lord is at hand; do not be anxious about anything, but in everything by prayer and supplication with thanksgiving let your requests be made known to God. And the peace of God, which surpasses all understanding, will guard your hearts and your minds in Christ Jesus.

> Finally, brothers, whatever is true, whatever is honorable, whatever is just, whatever is pure, whatever is lovely, whatever is commendable, if there is any excellence, if there is anything worthy of praise, think about these things. What you have learned and received and heard and seen in me— practice these things, and the God of peace will be with you. (Philippians 4:4–9)

God's peace stands guard over our hearts and minds. We don't have to muster it on our own—we can't. I think this passage gives us helpful ideas to help us redirect our thinking:

- Praise God for who He is and what He has done. Practice gratitude.
- Pray about everything. Turn your worrisome thoughts into prayers. Don't judge your thoughts; hand them over to God, and let Him help you sort out what is true.
- Pivot your thoughts. Turn your what-if thinking into what-is thinking, and focus on the truth of who God is and who you are in Him.

Discussion Question 46: How do you struggle with "what if" thinking? What promises from God can help you focus on what is true?

Discussion Question 47: What is one thing you can start right now to help you remember that the Lord is with you and gives you His peace?

SCRIPTURE PRAYER

In peace I will both lie down and sleep; for You alone, O LORD, make me dwell in safety. (Psalm 4:8)

BENEDICTION

The LORD bless you and keep you;
The LORD make His face to shine upon you and be gracious to you;
The LORD lift up His countenance upon you and give you peace. (Numbers 6:24–26)

Be in the presence of the One who gives you His perfect peace. He stands guard and will help you with your thoughts. Rest in His presence. Amen.

The History of God's People

- The first people sin, and God promises them a Savior.
- God calls Abram/Abraham to be the Father of many nations.
- Abraham and Sarah have Isaac.
- Isaac and Rebecca have Esau and Jacob.
- God renames Jacob as Israel.
- Joseph is sold into slavery by his brothers.
- Joseph becomes second-in-command over Egypt and saves his family from famine.
- Jacob's family settles into the land of Egypt, and four hundred years later, they are slaves.
- Moses frees the people from slavery and leads them out of Egypt.
- The Israelites are in the desert for forty years.
- Joshua is chosen to lead God's people into the Promised Land.
- God's people turn away from God and worship the false gods of other nations.
- God allows the other nations to come against His people.
- God's people repent and turn toward God.
- This pattern continues to happen over and over again.
- God sends the judges to help His people.

DAY 2: ISRAEL'S UNFAITHFULNESS AND GOD'S FAITHFULNESS

Shalom is mentioned one time in the Book of Judges. This word is used in reference to God's unending peace given to His children, despite their forgetfulness of God and what He had done for them.

READ JUDGES 2:11–23

As we read this passage, a little over three hundred years had passed since God led the Israelites out of Egypt under the leadership of Moses. God brought them out of slavery into the land of Canaan and gave them a life of freedom.

God rescued His people. God kept His promises to His people, and they were now living in the land of the promise in freedom. But instead of abiding in God's love, drawing closer to Him because of how He showed that love and provided for them, the Israelites wandered away from Him.

After Moses' successor, Joshua, died, the children of Israel chased after the false gods of Canaan:

- Baal, the god of storms, promised good crops, which was important for people dependent upon seasonal rains for survival.
- Asherah, the goddess of fertility and war, promised to give children and safeguard the Israelites in battle.

When we look at the history of God's people in the Bible, we see a cycle of sin and brokenness. God's people would stray, and then they would find themselves in horrific hardships; when they grew tired of the consequences, they would repent and cry out for the Lord to save them. The Scriptures reveal God's repeated mercy and compassion for His people. God would send another judge to lead the people. But Israel's repentance was short-lived, as again they returned to their false gods, forgetting they were God's children.

The Book of Judges isn't easy to read, because some of the stories are uncomfortably familiar. We, like the Israelites, turn to false gods. Money. Status. Security. These things always fail us, though. The Book of Judges provides a glimpse of God's grace and His never-ending mercy for His children. And because God knew our sinful nature would cloud our thinking, He gave us the Commandments so we would know His will for us. The first one deals with this issue:

The First Commandment
You shall have no other gods.

What does this mean?
We should fear, love, and trust in God above all things.[13]

When we examine the Ten Commandments and their meanings in the catechism, we discover that each says, "We should fear and love God," but the explanation of the First Commandment is the only one with the additional directive to "trust in God above all things."

Where do we really put our trust? Maybe, if you are like me, when considering this commandment, you think, *Since I don't have statues of false gods in my house, this isn't a problem for me.* But take a closer look at your life and ask, "Do I trust God above *all* things?"

What do you cling to for security or peace of mind? Family, friends, money, health, your job, or your own abilities? All these things seem stable on some level, but each can disappear or change in an instant, and none are certain. When we trust someone or something more than we trust God, it shows a misplaced faith and leads us into the same cycle of sin the Israelites struggled with.

Discussion Question 48: To what false gods do you cling?

THE CALL OF GIDEON

Once again, Israel did evil in the sight of the Lord, and as a consequence of their sin, He allowed the Midianites to oppress them for seven years. Whenever the Israelites planted their crops, the Midianites and others invaded the country. They stayed on the land, ruined the crops, and did not spare a living thing for Israel. They came like swarms of locusts, so many that it was impossible to count them. The Israelites became so impoverished by Midian that they cried out to the Lord.

> Now the angel of the Lord came and sat under the terebinth at Ophrah, which belonged to Joash the Abiezrite, while his son Gideon was beating out wheat in the winepress to hide it from the Midianites. And the angel of the Lord appeared to him and said to him, "The Lord is with you, O mighty man of valor."
>
> And Gideon said to him, "Please, my lord, if the Lord is with us, why then has all this happened to us? And where are all His wonderful deeds that our fathers recounted to us, saying, 'Did not the Lord bring us up from Egypt?' But now the Lord has forsaken us and given us into the hand of Midian." (Judges 6:11–13)

After reading this part of the story, consider the following points:

- The Angel of the Lord is Jesus.
- We have no indication that Gideon is a mighty man of valor or warrior (as some translations read), yet that is what Jesus calls him, foreshadowing Gideon's future.
- At this point, it's not clear if Gideon realizes he is talking to the Lord, because of the way he questions if the Lord is really with them.

> And the Lord turned to him and said, "Go in this might of yours and save Israel from the hand of Midian; do not I send you?" And he said to Him, "Please, Lord, how can I save Israel? Behold, my clan is the weakest in Manasseh, and I am the least in my father's house." And the Lord said to him, "But I will be with you, and you shall strike the Midianites as one man." And he said to Him, "If now I have found favor in Your eyes, then show me a sign that it is You who speak with

me. Please do not depart from here until I come to You and bring out my present and set it before You." And He said, "I will stay till you return." (Judges 6:14–18)

When I read this passage, I was amazed that Gideon questioned the Lord, but then I remembered that I question God all the time.

Discussion Question 49: How have you questioned God? Does it seem different because you do not see Him face-to-face like Gideon did?

The Lord was patient with Gideon, even when he asked for a sign to prove He is God:

> So Gideon went into his house and prepared a young goat and unleavened cakes from an ephah of flour. The meat he put in a basket, and the broth he put in a pot, and brought them to him under the terebinth and presented them. And the angel of God said to him, "Take the meat and the unleavened cakes, and put them on this rock, and pour the broth over them." And he did so. Then the angel of the LORD reached out the tip of the staff that was in His hand and touched the meat and the unleavened cakes. And fire sprang up from the rock and consumed the meat and the unleavened cakes. And the angel of the LORD vanished from his sight. Then Gideon perceived that He was the angel of the LORD. And Gideon said, "Alas, O Lord GOD! For now I have seen the angel of the LORD face to face." But the LORD said to him, "Peace be to you. Do not fear; you shall not die." Then Gideon built an altar there to the LORD and called it, The LORD Is Peace. To this day it still stands at Ophrah, which belongs to the Abiezrites. (Judges 6:19–24)

When we meet Gideon in this story, he is hiding in a wine vat, getting the grain from the wheat. The Midianites had been stealing their food for seven years.

The Israelites did not gain peace from the empty promises of their false gods, because true peace comes only from the one true God.

Despite Gideon's fear, doubts, and questions about God, Jesus came to sit with him. We see only love from Jesus toward Gideon. He is patient and shows kindness.

Gideon saw God face-to-face, and in His presence, he received peace. He built an altar and called it, "The LORD Is Peace." Gideon received from Jesus what he could not receive from the false gods.

In the Divine Service, you and I stand in the presence of God with our weaknesses, and we receive His peace through the Word and in the Holy Supper. The Lord also gives us His strength and forgiveness of sins.

How do you need Jesus to be your peace today?

How has God been patient with you throughout your struggles with trust, faith, and peace in His presence?

Day 3: The Lord Calls Gideon

Now may the Lord of peace Himself give you peace at all times in every way. The Lord be with you all. (2 Thessalonians 3:16)

Today we continue to look at the story of Gideon. Take notice of how God deals with his fears and questions.

READ JUDGES 6:25–32

The Lord told Gideon to destroy the altar of Baal that his father built. Gideon was too afraid of his family and of the men of his town, so he and ten of his men went during the night, under the cover of darkness and while the townspeople slept, to destroy the altar.

In those brief verses, God gives us a glimpse of Gideon and his struggle with fear. He called Gideon a mighty warrior, yet He also allows us to see his fearfulness.

God gives you a new identity too. Your reality or actions don't create God's view of you. Your worth is based upon who you are in Him. You're His beloved. You are God's daughter. In your new identity, you are able to fulfill the vocations God has called you to do, even the ones for which you do not feel qualified. God will equip you to do what might feel impossible:

- Caring for elderly parents
- Providing care for a sick spouse or a child facing a serious illness
- Traveling as a missionary through a place where Christians are persecuted
- Standing up for the truth in your work place, even when you stand alone

What vocations or callings might you add to this list?

Discussion Question 50: When have you felt brave and fearful at the same time?

What altars have you built that need to come down? Are you more concerned about what others may think than what God thinks? Explain.

The Lord told Gideon he would save Israel from the hand of Midian. We've already read about how Gideon asked Him for a sign (Judges 6:17). Gideon would go on to ask God two more times for a sign.

> Then Gideon said to God, "If You will save Israel by my hand, as You have said, behold, I am laying a fleece of wool on the threshing floor. If there is dew on the fleece alone, and it is dry on all the ground, then I shall know that You will save Israel by my hand, as You have said." And it was so. When he rose early next morning and squeezed the fleece, he wrung enough dew from the fleece to fill a bowl with water. Then Gideon said to God, "Let not Your anger burn against me; let me speak just once more. Please let me test just once more with the fleece. Please let it be dry on the fleece only, and on all the ground let there be dew." And God did so that night; and it was dry on the fleece only, and on all the ground there was dew. (Judges 6:36–40)

In Judges 6, Gideon tested God three times. Notice how God responded to him—He didn't get angry. God showed love, patience, and compassion toward Gideon.

Gideon focused on his limitations and wondered how he would accomplish what God has asked him to do. We might find ourselves thinking, "How could Gideon question God?" But if we think it through, we realize that we, too, focus on our limitations and forget the promises God has made to us.

God was teaching Gideon that he could trust Him above all things.

What promises from God do you struggle to believe?

AGAINST ALL ODDS

Gideon gathered thirty-two thousand warriors to fight against the

Midianites, but God told him he didn't need that many. At God's direction, Gideon reduced his troops to three hundred. This way, the Lord would show that the victory over the Midianites was due to His strength and might and not due to the efforts of men.

Gideon wrestled with his fears. He had tested God three times, and each time God showed Gideon the truth. That should have been enough, but the anxious thoughts pushed their way to the surface. Gideon wondered, "How can I defeat the Midianites when they outnumber us 450 to 1?"

> That same night the LORD said to him, "Arise, go down against the camp, for I have given it into your hand. But if you are afraid to go down, go down to the camp with Purah your servant. And you shall hear what they say, and afterward your hands shall be strengthened to go down against the camp." Then he went down with Purah his servant to the outposts of the armed men who were in the camp. And the Midianites and the Amalekites and all the people of the East lay along the valley like locusts in abundance, and their camels were without number, as the sand that is on the seashore in abundance. When Gideon came, behold, a man was telling a dream to his comrade. And he said, "Behold, I dreamed a dream, and behold, a cake of barley bread tumbled into the camp of Midian and came to the tent and struck it so that it fell and turned it upside down, so that the tent lay flat." And his comrade answered, "This is no other than the sword of Gideon the son of Joash, a man of Israel; God has given into his hand Midian and all the camp." (Judges 7:9–14)

Did you notice what God said to Gideon? "If you are afraid, . . . go." He didn't rebuke Gideon for his fears. Yahweh met Gideon in his fear and showed him, once again, who He is.

I want you to underline the sentence that starts with "And the Midianites . . ." (v. 12). Think about how you would have felt if you were Gideon, with an army of three hundred against a gigantic army without number?

Discussion Question 51: Are you surprised by the patience and compassion God had for Gideon? Why or why not?

Gideon was now ready. It's not clear from the story if God gave Gideon a battle plan, but the strategy Gideon used was effective. He divided the three hundred men into three companies, and he made sure each man had a trumpet and an empty jar with a torch inside. They advanced under the cover of darkness, which was crucial to the plan so the Midianites would not see how scarce they were in number. The three hundred swords of the Israelite army could not defeat a massive opponent the size of the Midianite army. But the Midianites heard trumpets blowing, jars smashing, and shouting all around them, and they saw the torches burning. This made it appear like they were surrounded.

Because of the dream and its interpretation, God ignited panic in the hearts of the Midianites. Panicked people do not think logically. The Lord set every Midianite's sword against his comrades. They fled, and the Israelites pursued them. God won the battle for the Israelites that day. It was by His hand and strength that they were victorious.

For the next forty years, Gideon was the judge of Israel. But as had happened so many times before, Gideon led the people to worship other gods, and God's people once again did evil in the sight of the Lord and served other gods. The cycle continued.

In your journal time today, abide in the peace that is yours through faith in Christ Jesus' work in your life and in the lives of your loved ones.

Day 4: Jesus Gives Us His Peace

Jesus descended into this broken world to save you from your sins and give you His peace. Read that sentence again. God the Son left the perfect peace of heaven to come to the chaos of life on earth to give you His peace.

> For to us a child is born, to us a son is given; and the government shall be upon His shoulder, and His name shall be called Wonderful Counselor, Mighty God, Everlasting Father, Prince of Peace. (Isaiah 9:6)

Does peace feel distant, like it's always out of reach? The harder you try to obtain it, the more elusive it becomes. We've all seen headlines of articles claiming, "Five steps to inner peace." When we click the link, hoping to find something helpful, we discover the advice is at best a temporary fix for an existential problem. Techniques and tips that tell us what we should do put pressure on us, and that's the opposite of peace.

Discussion Question 52: Where do you search for peace?

Maybe, if you are like me, your mind gets stuck in circumstances. We experience friction at work, conflict at home, and bedlam in the world. Even if our lives are not complicated, we must move between these areas, and doing so with a mindset of peacefulness is difficult. The only way to achieve peacefulness is to reset our minds to focus on the only One who brings us peace.

> You keep him in perfect peace whose mind is stayed on You, because he trusts in You. (Isaiah 26:3)

It's important for us to understand that peace isn't something we will have when we finally get everything figured out. It's available right here and now, because Jesus wants to be our peace.

As we look at the life of Jesus in Scripture, His life was not always what we would call peaceful. None of us will ever experience the kind of warfare Jesus endured on earth, yet we can have peace because He provides it. Jesus shows again and again that the path to peace includes confident prayer.

Jesus talked to God. He would often go to quiet places to pray and be in communion with His Father, who poured out His peace upon His Son. Jesus knew He was the way of salvation for humanity through His sacrifice on the cross. Jesus never wavered—He trusted God above all things.

As we think about the events of Good Friday, let's focus on the words of Jesus. In the Garden of Gethsemane, He talked to His Father. Look at Luke 22:43–44, in which Jesus was in agony over what was about to happen. God's peace came in the form of an angel that ministered to Jesus. The Father's love poured out over Jesus, strengthening Him for what was to come. In a few hours, on the hill at Calvary, Jesus would hang in agony on the cross because that was the only way to earn our redemption.

Jesus had to suffer separation from God the Father for our sins. As He hung on the cross, Jesus was exiled in hell for our sins. We will never have to know what it's like to be separated from God, because Jesus did it for us. I cannot imagine anything worse than being separated from God.

Jesus prayed the words of Psalm 22:1, "My God, My God, why have You forsaken Me," while He was on the cross. He found comfort in talking to His Father. As a result, Jesus never lost trust in His Abba.

In His final words in Luke 23:46, "Father, into Your hands I commit My spirit!" we see Jesus turning Himself over to God the Father. He rested in Abba's perfect love for Him.

As we sit with these words and images of Jesus's death, we learn the peace He had on Good Friday is the same peace He gives to us.

As I've talked to women from all over the world, I have found these common circumstances that disturb our peace:

- Aging parents or loved ones
- Disagreements with a spouse on raising children and teaching them the faith

- Financial stress
- Children of all ages and stages
- Letting your child make mistakes
- Letting go of your adult children
- Family dynamics
- The death of a loved one, or their own death
- Marital problems
- Family and friends who do not know and trust Jesus

What would you add to this list? Which ones do you struggle with the most?

Whatever you face today that threatens your peace or causes anxiety to swell up within you, remember and take comfort knowing Jesus faced it for you on the cross. Every burden or sorrow we bear is because we live in a broken and sinful world, we ourselves are sinful, and Satan torments us.

Jesus knows and understands every trial humans will ever face. Jesus died for all of it.

You can rest in the presence of Jesus by spending time in His Word, being in fellowship with other Christians, and being in the Divine Service, through which Jesus comes to us in His body and blood. God blesses us with everything we will need to face each moment of our lives.

PEACE IN GOD'S WORD

One morning, when my alarm clock went off, I smacked the snooze button and put my head back down on the pillow, thinking sleep would be better than early morning Bible study. I was emotionally and spiritually exhausted from difficult life circumstances beyond my control. As I lay there, I wondered what would happen if I missed Bible study this one time. But I hauled myself out of bed, thanking the Holy Spirit for the nudge, and I went to see what awaited me in class.

That morning, we began a study of the Book of James. We spent the whole time looking at these verses:

> Count it all joy, my brothers, when you meet trials of various
> kinds, for you know that the testing of your faith produces
> steadfastness. And let steadfastness have its full effect, that

you may be perfect and complete, lacking in nothing. (James 1:2–4)

Now God had my attention. How in the world could I count it all joy when I faced the trials I was experiencing in my life? To be honest, at that time I didn't understand the difference between happiness and joy. Happiness depends upon our circumstances, while joy comes from knowing Jesus. In His presence, there is fullness of joy (see Psalm 16:11). There is peace in knowing that Jesus walks with us through everything. My faith was being tested, but God was working within me and giving me His steadfast strength.

Our discussions led to Romans 5:3–5. Look it up and fill in these blanks.

In what do you rejoice? _____

What does suffering produce? _____

What does endurance produce? _____

What does character produce? _____

Hope is poured into our hearts through the Holy Spirit, who dwells in our hearts. After studying those passages that morning, I knew why God woke me up. He wanted to spend time with me in the Word so He could fill me up.

As I drove to work after that class, I laughed with God. I told Him, "I feel like I have enough character already because of everything I am facing." Some people are shocked when I tell them I pray like that, but God knows my thoughts and understands my humor. It felt good to laugh with God and be in His presence in Bible study that morning. I knew He was with me and wasn't going to abandon me.

The trials I faced during that time didn't change because I went to Bible study. On the contrary—as the days went on, things got worse. But God gave me a precious gift during that study; He showed me I could receive peace in His presence, because He is Shalom.

Ground yourself in the peace that only God provides, trusting in His faith-fulness to you and dwelling in His Word. Reflect on a time in your life when you have been surrounded by God's peace.

Day 5: When Church Hurts

Troy and I made a painful decision to leave our congregation. We had agonized over the complexity of a situation that led two hundred other members to leave as well. All of us were devastated, both those who chose to stay at the church and those of us who left. When one part of the Body of Christ hurts, we all hurt.

We found a sister congregation at which God gave us the comfort we needed for our grieving and weary souls. The pastor was kind and caring. The congregation opened their hearts and pews to new members, and we settled in.

Troy and I missed our former congregation, but after all that had happened, we didn't think it would be possible to go back. Then, when we had been away for two and a half years, we met Pastor Keith, the new pastor, at a social gathering. He asked questions and listened to our story. Then he asked, "When are you going to come home?"

Surprised, I said, "I don't know if that is possible. I don't know if we would be welcomed by everyone there." He assured us the invitation to come back home was always open.

Hope stirred in our hearts, and we began to pray about returning to our home church. Some would be happy to welcome us back, but there were those who would not want us to return. The heartache hadn't begun to heal for everyone.

The devil wants us to stay away from the Church, and he causes conflict among brothers and sisters in Christ. He seeks to demolish and dismantle the Body of believers, because he doesn't want us to receive the precious gifts of God in the Word and in the Sacraments.

We decided to return to our home congregation, and during our first weeks back, Pastor Keith preached a sermon series on reconciliation. One phrase during a sermon caught me off guard, and I found myself getting angry. "In God's eyes, it doesn't matter who is right or wrong; He asks us to forgive." Pastor talked about how every side had been hurt by what had happened. All I had been able to see was the wrong that had been done to my family and me. I was angered and hurt by losing our church family, and I grieved that things would never be the same. Whenever I talked about what happened, resentment clung to every word.

The heartache we experienced was real, but I had not understood the pain experienced by others involved. Satan unleashed his fury upon our church, and every person's heart had been broken. We all mourned our losses.

> For we do not wrestle against flesh and blood, but against
> the rulers, against the authorities, against the cosmic powers
> over this present darkness, against the spiritual forces of evil
> in the heavenly places. (Ephesians 6:12)

As we continued to assimilate back into the church we loved, there were relationships I doubted could ever be repaired. It took a while, but God mended those broken bonds.

Throughout this study, you've read about the gifts we receive at church. If those words have caused you to cringe and think, "Michelle, you cannot understand how painful it is for me to go to church. You have no idea how I've suffered," then you are right. I don't know what you've experienced. I am sorry for what has caused you stinging pain. But I have also been hurt at church. As a church worker, I have witnessed stories unfold that have tremendous heartache and harm. I feel anguish in the pit of my stomach because I know someone is hurting from a problem originating in the house of God, by the people of God.

Your tears carry a story that only God knows, and He meets you in each tear and holds you while you weep.

Discussion Question 53: What makes attending church hard for you?

Divisions among the members of our church family leave us with holes in our hearts, sanctuaries, Sunday School classes, and social gatherings. They leave us broken, shattered, and split. Friendships fade or even end. Sometimes, these walking wounded find a new church home at which they are fed spiritually and emotionally. But sometimes those who have been hurt decide going to church is too complicated; they worship God in their own way, or they fall away from God completely.

You may bear deep scars if the Church has hurt you, but I ask you the same question Pastor Keith asked us: When will you come home?

God will never leave you or forsake you, and His love for you never ends. He longs for you to be in church every time the doors open for worship. He seeks you relentlessly in the same way the shepherd sought his lost lamb. He has set the Table for you, a lavish banquet that restores you to Him and nourishes your faith. Jesus, your God of peace, offers you His body and blood, given and shed for you. He provides forgiveness of sins and strength to sustain you for the days ahead. God gives you His Holy Word, which bolsters your faith, encourages your heart, and assures you of His promise of salvation through Jesus. He also gives you brothers and sisters in Christ—a fellowship so sweet it gives a faint glimpse of the gifts promised in eternity.

True, the Church is filled with broken sinners, and we experience and cause pain, but if we keep our eyes on our Redeemer, we will share in the beauty of Him mending our hearts together.

Sometimes church is hard for other reasons. I asked some of my friends what makes church hard for them.

- Wrestling with kids
- Death of a loved one
- Holidays when you are missing family members
- When you go to church by yourself
- Disagreement with another church member
- When your spouse or adult children refuse to come to church

All these cause pain. What would you add to the list?

Every time I've struggled to go to church, I've asked God to help me, and His Holy Spirit meets me where I am and draws me to Him. The peace of His presence surrounds and strengthens me.

Discussion Question 54: What is your favorite part of the worship service? Why?

> And let the peace of Christ rule in your hearts, to which indeed you were called in one body. And be thankful. Let the word of Christ dwell in you richly, teaching and admonishing one another in all wisdom, singing psalms and hymns and spiritual songs, with thankfulness in your hearts to God. And whatever you do, in word or deed, do everything in the name of the Lord Jesus, giving thanks to God the Father through Him. (Colossians 3:15–17)

God uses your current situation to draw you closer to Him and to teach you about His peace. Spend some time today in reflection and prayer, asking Him to draw near to you in the places in your life you most need His peace.

WEEK 6 GROUP STUDY QUESTIONS

SHALOM

Shalom: *God is peace*

Pronunciation: *Shaw-lome'*

Used first by Gideon in Judges 6:24, Shalom describes the peace, completeness, harmony, and absence of conflict found only in God. Having asked for signs from God, and receiving them, Gideon was visited by an angel who spoke as the Lord Himself. Only Moses and Abraham had had such visitations. Bolstered in his faith, Gideon recognized that the Lord had been with the Israelites all along. So he built an altar at Ophrah, naming it "Shalom" as a reminder of God's presence, protection, and provision. When we learn that the Lord is Shalom, we remember that our peace is from Him alone.

Bible Verse: *"And the peace of God, which surpasses all understanding, will guard your hearts and your minds in Christ Jesus." (Philippians 4:7)*

REFLECTIONS

- What story stood out to you the most from this week's lessons? Why?
- What did you learn about God as the One who provides true peace?

DISCUSSION QUESTIONS

46. How do struggle with "what if" thinking? What promises from God can help you focus on what is true?

47. What is one thing you can start right now to help you remember that the Lord is with you and gives you His peace?

48. To what false gods do you cling?

49. How have you questioned God? Does it seem different because you do not see Him face-to-face like Gideon did?

50. When have you felt brave and fearful at the same time?

51. Are you surprised by the patience and compassion God had for Gideon? Why or why not?

52. Where do you search for peace?

53. What makes attending church hard for you?

54. What is your favorite part of the worship service? Why?

BENEDICTION

The LORD bless you and keep you;
The LORD make His face to shine upon you and be gracious
to you;
The LORD lift up His countenance upon you and give you
peace. (Numbers 6:24–26)

Yahweh Ra'ah

Yahweh Ra'ah: *The Lord is my Shepherd*

Pronunciation: *Ya-way raw-aw'*

This name of God is based on Psalm 23 and adapted from a Hebrew verb, ro'iy, meaning "to shepherd." It calls to mind the One who faithfully provides for His flock and who meets their every need. Jesus called Himself our Good Shepherd, who watches over us constantly, protects from danger, and leads us to shelter in His presence. He is intimate with His people. In other words, He is a friend.

Bible Verse: *"The LORD is my shepherd; I shall not want." (Psalm 23:1)*

DAY 1: JESUS, THE GOOD SHEPHERD, CARRIES YOU

Fear paralyzes a sheep when it is lost. It cries until the shepherd comes. But even when it is rescued, the sheep remains panic-stricken and unable to move. The shepherd gently lays the sheep across his shoulders and carries it home.

Perhaps you have seen an illustration of Jesus carrying a lamb across His shoulders or in His arms. The Early Christian Church loved this portrayal of Jesus. When the catacombs under Rome were discovered, paintings and murals of Jesus painted in this way were found.

Envision yourself as the lamb. Notice how close your face is to Jesus as He cradles you. He can turn and listen to you, and you can hear His voice in response. Tuck this image into your heart as we go through Psalm 23. Rather than thinking about it as a Scripture passage, think about it as a nearby place where sheep and shepherds roam. This psalm is a song about you! The Shepherd laid down His life for you and claimed you as His beloved child when you were baptized.

May the image of Jesus carrying you settle deep into your soul and bring you comfort. The Good Shepherd invites you to find rest in the peace of His presence. The familiar words of Psalm 23 are woven into the very fabric of your being by the One who knit you together in your mother's womb. The promises written about in this psalm are etched upon your heart and belong to you forever. These promises are far greater than any difficulty you face now or in the future. The Good Shepherd will gently lead you, carry you, and sustain you through this life and into eternity with Him.

THE GOOD SHEPHERD LEADS THROUGH THE STORM

Lights twinkled in the tree and the fire hissed slowly, punctuated with sharp crackles and pops. Sitting there, cozy and warm, was the perfect way to unwind from a Christmas week that was markedly different from the others in my memory. A quiet conversation with Troy added to the tranquility.

My body was recovering from parathyroid surgery, and I needed time to repair and rest. Suddenly, pain exploded through my chest as my heart seemed to hammer its way out. Troy sprang into action and called my sister-in-law, who lived down the road, to come watch the boys. We headed for the emergency room.

In a follow-up appointment earlier that day, the doctor had said my heart rate was elevated. He suspected my thyroid was irritated from the surgery and was releasing hormones that caused my heart to beat faster.

The ER team sprang into action as soon as they heard the word *heart*. I relayed the doctor's assumptions to the team, and they confirmed them through blood tests. There wasn't much they could do for me. My body had to go through the process of healing and wait for my thyroid to calm down.

We headed home hopeful, thinking the worst was behind us. But I endured several excruciating hours that night, and the next morning, because I couldn't handle the pain any longer, I pleaded for my doctor to arrange an appointment with an endocrinologist. He agreed and got me an appointment for that same morning. It was good that he did.

"Michelle," the endocrinologist told me, "your thyroid is dumping dangerous amounts of hormones into your blood, causing your heart rate and blood pressure to skyrocket to alarming levels. Your thyroid has created a life-threatening storm inside your body, and we need to get you to the hospital right away."

Cold sweat trickled down my spine and my mind swirled as I tried to grasp what was going on inside my body.

At the hospital, the nurse gasped at my vitals. Her eyes grew round with alarm, and she ran from the room to get help. I felt too sick to process how I was feeling, and the nurse's actions made things worse. My eyes filled with tears and I grabbed Troy's hand.

"Help me, Jesus," I prayed.

I knew my condition was serious, but now I understood my condition could be life-threatening. The endocrinologist and a team of cardiac specialists determined the ICU was the safest place to monitor my heart until the thyroid storm ended. However, there was nothing they could do to fix it; my body had to wait it out. The kind treatment from the doctors and nurses and knowing that my heart was monitored constantly brought me comfort. What brought me true peace, though, was resting in the love of my Good Shepherd. I knew He held me in His capable hands. The Good Shepherd was able to comfort Troy and our boys in a way I could not.

All I could do was wait and rest as the thyroid storm subsided. I continued to see my doctor over the next few months. And when she released me from her care, we both hoped I would never see her again.

Life seldom follows our plans.

How does your life look different from what you planned?

Psalm 23 is one of the most beloved passages of Scripture. We often associate it with the end of life, but let's look at it as a guide through all of life.

David carried a shepherd's staff long before he wore a king's crown. Shepherds continually watched over their sheep. When night fell, they found a place to corral their flock. When the shepherd slept, he would position himself as the gate to the pen. Any wild animal or person wishing to harm the sheep had to get past the shepherd.

The Good Shepherd cares about every detail of your life. His love for you is enough to see you through each moment. Whatever you face today, friend, know that having the Lord for your Shepherd is enough to get you through each minute, hour, and day.

The LORD is my shepherd; I shall not want. (Psalm 23:1)

Let's look at the language of the first verse. Notice the pronoun *my*. This is different from saying, "The Lord is our shepherd"; the word *my* makes it personal. Note, too, the verb in the present tense. This isn't a future state;

it's current and active. You are in the presence of your Good Shepherd right now.

Discussion Question 55: How does knowing that the Good Shepherd is present for your every heartbeat make a difference in your day?

The second part of the verse is a statement of fulfillment. Since Jesus is your guide and provider, you have everything you need each minute. There is nothing else you need.

SCRIPTURE PRAYER

He will tend His flock like a shepherd; He will gather the lambs in His arms;

He will carry them in His bosom, and gently lead those that are with young. (Isaiah 40:11)

BENEDICTION

The LORD bless you and keep you;
The LORD make His face to shine upon you and be gracious to you;
The LORD lift up His countenance upon you and give you peace. (Numbers 6:24–26)

You are always in the presence of the Good Shepherd. When you draw near to Him, you receive Him in the Gospel message and in His Holy Meal. He guides you and provides everything you need. Rest in His protective embrace. His love for you is tender and true, and it will endure forever.

DAY 2: THE GOOD SHEPHERD KNOWS YOU

He makes me lie down in green pastures. He leads me beside still waters. (Psalm 23:2)

Sheep are difficult creatures. They drink only from still water. They rest only when all their needs are met. They wander away, and since they have poor eyesight, they can't find their way back to the flock. They aren't inclined to lie down, so they must be made to rest. The shepherd, however, knows how to handle sheep and how to provide for them.

THE GOOD SHEPHERD STILLS THE STORM

On that day, when evening had come, He said to them, "Let us go across to the other side." And leaving the crowd, they took Him with them in the boat, just as He was. And other boats were with Him. And a great windstorm arose, and the waves were breaking into the boat, so that the boat was already filling. But He was in the stern, asleep on the cushion. And they woke Him and said to Him, "Teacher, do You not care that we are perishing?" And He awoke and rebuked the wind and said to the sea, "Peace! Be still!" And the wind ceased, and there was a great calm. He said to them, "Why are you so afraid? Have you still no faith?" And they were filled with great fear and said to one another, "Who then is this, that even the wind and the sea obey Him?" (Mark 4:35–41)

The Sea of Galilee is set among the hills of northern Israel, seven hundred feet below sea level. Storms come up quick and furious, and because of the surrounding hills, the wind creates a funneling effect, causing the storms to become violent in an instant.

If you haven't seen it, take some time to look up Rembrandt's painting, "The Storm on the Sea of Galilee." Look closely, and you will notice that the artist has painted himself into the boat. Even though the story is about the disciples in the boat with Jesus, we all have faced storms and life circumstances we did not choose. Rembrandt lost three of his children in infancy and one in childbirth, and he also lost his wife. He knew the storms of life, and he put himself in that painting as a reminder that Jesus was with him in the storm.

Your Good Shepherd carries you through turbulent and tumultuous circumstances as well. Amid the howling winds and raging waters, Jesus says, "Peace, be still." The storm may not stop, but His words are meant for you. No matter what is happening around you, Jesus is your peace.

Discussion Question 56: Where in your life do you need the peace of Jesus today?

> The position of this Psalm is worthy of notice. It follows the twenty-second, which is peculiarly the Psalm of the Cross. There are no green pastures, no still waters on the other side of the twenty-second psalm. It is only after we have read, "My God, my God, why hast thou forsaken me?" that we come to "The Lord is my Shepherd." We must by experience know the value of blood-shedding, and see the sword awakened against the Shepherd, before we shall be able truly to know the Sweetness of the good Shepherd's care.[14]

We know the love of the Shepherd because of the salvation He won for us on the cross. The pastures are restful and green because of the peace that comes from His presence and His Word.

At times, our lives are filled with storms, and we long for the stillness that comes after, but sometimes the storms are not stilled. Nevertheless, we can rest even as the storms rage because we receive peace in His arms.

THE GOOD SHEPHERD LEADS
US THROUGH THE UNEXPECTED

Remember the doctor I hoped never to see again? I developed kidney stones, and blood tests revealed that my parathyroid levels were still too high.

That doctor said, "It looks like you'll need to have surgery again, and there is a possibility you might lose your remaining parathyroids. You can live without them, but it will create some challenges."

For this surgery, I was placed into the hands of a highly skilled surgeon who had been successful in helping others keep their parathyroid function. Because my vitamin D levels were dangerously low, I had to wait several months so they could be built up so surgery would be safe.

One night, during that time of waiting, I was tucking Jacob and Matthew into bed. Usually, Matthew is all snuggly and full of hugs and kisses. His beautiful big blue eyes, which usually danced with mischief and fun, were brimming with tears. I pulled him close and asked if he was okay. With his eyes turned down, he shrugged his tiny shoulders. Finally, his little lips quivered, and he said, "Mommy, I don't want you to die."

I gave him a big hug and kiss and told him I wasn't planning to die anytime soon. By then, both Jacob and Matthew had tears spilling down their cheeks. I asked Matthew, "Why do you think I'm going to die?"

He looked at me very seriously and said, "All of your vitamins are falling out of you."

My perceptive little guy had heard me on the phone with my doctors. I realized I should have been explaining more about my health issues to my boys. Pulling them both onto my lap, I told them the truth. "Someday, death will come to all of us. It will make us sad, but we needn't be afraid. Jesus is always with us. Here on earth and in heaven, Jesus is with us. And Jesus loves us, so He will take us to heaven, where no one is sick and no one is sad."

Concern filled Jacob's face, and he told me he still felt yucky on the inside and didn't want me to be sick anymore.

"Worry makes us feel sick on the inside, and it doesn't make things better." I told him we can give our fears to God and let Him take care of them.

Jacob wanted to pray about it, and so we did. I prayed first, then Jacob. When it was Matthew's turn, Jacob urged, "Matthew, it's your turn."

Matthew replied, "I'm not worried anymore. Jesus will take care of it. I'm sleepy."

My older son, Jacob, said he knew Jesus would take care of me, but he wanted to give Him the worries physically. I held his hands and said, "Pretend your worries are in your heart. Take them out of you and fling them up to heaven." So Jacob and I flung our worries up to heaven into the loving hands of God. "Remember, sweetheart, it's important not to take the worries back. Let God take care of them." He hugged me and assured me he felt much better. I felt better too, knowing that God is my Shepherd.

My conversation with my boys reminded me of an important truth— my soul could rest in the Good Shepherd. After surgery, the conversation with my sons continued to encourage me as I learned to live without my parathyroid function.

Casting all your anxieties on Him, because He cares for you. (1 Peter 5:7)

What burdens do you need to cast upon your Good Shepherd?

The Good Shepherd calls you to Himself and provides you with the shelter you need. In your journal time today, spend time in thanksgiving to God for carrying your burdens.

Day 3: He Restores My Soul

He restores my soul. He leads me in paths of righteousness for His name's sake. (Psalm 23:3)

In this verse, King David is talking about being lost in sin and desperate for a Savior. Like the sheep who got lost and stuck in fear, we also were stuck in our sin and could not loosen the grip of separation and death the devil held over us.

We aren't sinners because we sin. We sin because we are sinners.

Sin is the disease. It's the infection and corruption of the human heart. The heart, which should run to God, runs instead to created things. Corrupted by sin, the heart fears, loves, and trusts in anything but God. Because of our first parents' decision to eat the forbidden fruit, all of our hearts are corrupted by sin. This corruption creates havoc in our lives.

> The Gospel is the antidote to this condition. The One who never was plagued by "me, me, me" gave Himself selflessly so that we might be united with Him in spite of ourselves.[15]

Jesus was born without sin. Jesus was not contaminated by the same sinful nature we have inherited. The Good Shepherd stepped into the brokenness of this world and set His face toward Calvary because our lives depended upon it. We could not rescue or save ourselves. There wasn't a sacrifice we could offer to make payment for our sin.

Our sins were nailed to the cross with Jesus—He had to suffer and die to pay the penalty. Even if we wanted to take Jesus' place on the cross, it wouldn't have been enough to pay for our sins, let alone the sins of the whole world. God Himself had to step into human history, fully man and fully God, to save His people from their sins.

Your soul has been brought back and restored so that you might live for eternity in the presence of the Good Shepherd.

Jesus restored you in your Baptism.

> What shall we say then? Are we to continue in sin that grace may abound? By no means! How can we who died to sin still live in it? Do you not know that all of us who have been baptized into Christ Jesus were baptized into His death? We were buried therefore with Him by baptism into death, in order that, just as Christ was raised from the dead by the glory of the Father, we too might walk in newness of life. (Romans 6:1–4)

You have been made new. Your Shepherd will lead you on the right paths because of who He is—the Good Shepherd. He will never forsake you; He will never abandon you to wander hopelessly, helplessly without Him.

> Even though I walk through the valley of the shadow of death, I will fear no evil, for you are with me; Your rod and Your staff, they comfort me. (Psalm 23:4)

This world is the valley of the shadow of death, yet God promises you need not fear evil or death, because you are in the presence of the Good Shepherd. You and I will face the death of loved ones, and the people we love will face our death someday. The Good Shepherd will guide us from this life into eternity.

These passages from God's Word bring us peace as we think about death.

> If we live, we live to the Lord, and if we die, we die for the Lord. So then, whether we live or whether we die, we are the Lord's. (Romans 14:8)

> "O death, where is your victory? O death, where is your sting?" The sting of death is sin, and the power of sin is the law. But thanks be to God, who gives us the victory through our Lord Jesus Christ. (1 Corinthians 15:55–57)

The shepherd's rod was a weapon used to protect the sheep from wild animals. We read about how David had killed a lion and a bear (see 1 Samuel 17:34–35). Biblical scholars believe he used the rod to club it over the head. Shepherds also used the staff for stability while walking through dangerous terrain. The hook on the end snagged sheep out of pits or from the water. The rod and the staff symbolize God's strength and protection for us.

Our Good Shepherd walks with us. When we face evil, He guides us through to safety. He guides us by His Word, our source of knowledge about God and His kingdom. We cannot overcome evil by our own effort. Jesus Himself is our strength and protection. Jesus defeated evil for us. By the Word of God, we know Him and His promises.

> You prepare a table before me in the presence of my enemies.
> (Psalm 23:5a)

The Shepherd invites you to the table of the Lord's Supper to receive His gifts of forgiveness and strength. These gifts are delivered to you every time your church offers the Holy Supper to sustain your faith. The evil one is reminded of his defeat as we join in the feast of victory of the Lamb of God, who grants us His peace.

> You anoint my head with oil. (Psalm 23:5b)

The shepherd would carefully check each sheep at the end of the day for cuts and scrapes and pour oil on the cuts for healing. Without the oil, flies could lay their eggs in the wounds, and parasites would drive the sheep mad. The shepherd would also put the oil in the sheep's nostrils to protect it from being bitten by little snakes. The smell of the oil repelled such predators. Additionally, anointing a person with oil was a soothing, welcoming act meant as a blessing for an honored guest.

God anoints us with His Word. Negative thoughts can plague our minds and take over and drive us mad. Our Lord invites us to dwell in His Word, where He reveals His true nature as our holy, loving Father.

> My cup overflows. (Psalm 23:5c)

During this time in history, a host would keep a visitor's cup full as an indication that the visitor was welcome to stay. When the host wanted to communicate it was time for the visitor to leave, he would stop filling the visitor's cup. David's words here are an acknowledgment of God's abundant provision, of His overflowing grace and love. God continuously pours out His blessings on us and never stops providing them. Of that, we can be certain.

Your Good Shepherd wants you in His presence all the time. He carries you close to Himself, constantly protecting and guiding you. God's blessings to you overflow. You cannot hold them back or stop them from coming. The Good Shepherd loves you and longs to spend time with you.

Discussion Question 57: How does knowing that the Good Shepherd walks with you through the valley of the shadow of death bring you comfort?

Discussion Question 58: Where do you see the blessings from God overflowing in your life?

Reflect on Psalm 23, and receive the Means of Grace—Word and Sacrament—that the Good Shepherd provides. In your journal time, spend some time thanking your Good Shepherd for His tender care for you.

DAY 4: LOST AND FOUND

God paints the picture of the Good Shepherd for us in Psalm 23, and Ezekiel 34 points toward the Shepherd who will come to save His flock.

> I Myself will be the shepherd of My sheep, and I Myself will
> make them lie down, declares the Lord GOD. (Ezekiel 34:15)

READ EZEKIEL 34

In this passage, God addresses the bad shepherds of His people. They did not take care of His flock as God had commanded. Verse 16 discusses how the Shepherd will seek the lost and bring back those who have strayed. God will step into history to restore His flock, find the lost sheep, and be their Shepherd.

In Luke 15, we see the Pharisees and scribes upset because Jesus associated with sinners and ate with them. The Pharisees were all about following rules and laws; they made morality their religion. They set themselves apart from everyone else because they believed following all their laws made them holy and better than other people. Their self-importance became more crucial than pointing the people to the Messiah and saving those who were lost. They failed to acknowledge that they were sinners too.

The Pharisees were concerned with saving themselves. They relied more upon their human effort than on what God wanted to do for them.

In response to the Pharisees, Jesus told a parable that consisted of three short stories. He wanted the Pharisees to know who He was and why He had come. In our session on Abba, we focused on the third story of this chapter, the parable of the prodigal son. Today, we focus on the lost sheep.

> What man of you, having a hundred sheep, if he has lost one
> of them, does not leave the ninety-nine in the open country,

and go after the one that is lost, until he finds it? And when he has found it, he lays it on his shoulders, rejoicing. And when he comes home, he calls together his friends and his neighbors, saying to them, "Rejoice with me, for I have found my sheep that was lost." Just so, I tell you, there will be more joy in heaven over one sinner who repents than over ninety-nine righteous persons who need no repentance. (Luke 15:4–7)

Jesus came for the sinner—the lost one. He came for you. Therefore, you can be certain that you have great value to the Shepherd. You matter to Him.

The self-righteous attitude of the Pharisees might cause us to be irritated by their harsh judgments toward sinners. We cannot fathom how they could hold such hypocritical self-importance. However, we fall into the trap of moralistic thinking too. It may not always be as blatant as that of the Pharisees, but it's there. We are as sinful as the scribes and Pharisees.

I struggle when shame causes me to reflect inward on my actions instead of looking outward toward the grace overflowing from the cross of Calvary.

God's love and mercy spill over and cover all our smelly, dirty, secret sins and remove them from us.

God has given us a precious gift in the part of the Divine Service called *Confession and Absolution.* We confess our sins before God, and the pastor absolves us of our sins. The absolution releases us from our sins and offers us forgiveness. The pastor can do this because he represents Jesus during the worship service—he is the messenger of Christ, called by God to preach, teach, and administer the Sacraments, among other ministry responsibilities.

We can come before God at any time and confess our sins and repent of them, and Jesus removes them from us.

Sometimes we get stuck in our sins. Think about a sin you struggle with. Maybe you feel separated from God because of it. Place yourself within this parable.

You are the lost sheep. You are stuck and afraid. You cry out to the Shepherd. He comes to you and rescues you. Ask Him to remove your sin from you. You do not need to hold on to that shame or sin any longer. It's not your burden to carry: the Shepherd will take it for you.

The Pharisees needed the Shepherd to rescue them from their morality because it had become destructive. God gives us His Law, the Commandments, to show us how He expects us to live our lives. His Law is complete—it covers all aspects of every life. The Pharisees and scribes thought they could improve on the Law, and so they added hundreds of rules that they believed made them more obedient and therefore more acceptable to God. They made being good their god.

But the religious leaders couldn't keep God's Law—no one can. They couldn't even keep their own laws perfectly. Jesus called them out on this, and they didn't like that.

Look at the story again. Jesus was physically present among the religious leaders. He was with them, there to guide them back to Himself with the parable that served as His rod and staff. The Good Shepherd is with us as well. He seeks us, calling to us in His Word. He welcomes us back to His Table. It's tempting to see ourselves as separated because of our sin, but Jesus closed that distance on His cross.

King David penned Psalm 51 after being confronted with his sin of adultery with Bathsheba and with causing the death of her husband, Uriah. You can read more about this story in 2 Samuel 11–12.

READ PSALM 51

This is a penitential psalm. David confesses and repents with heart-wrenching honesty. Like David, our souls are like the parched, dry ground, dusty and full of cracks. But our merciful God pours His steadfast love over us and fills in where we need it most. There is no sin so great that the blood of Christ cannot cover it.

The Good Shepherd creates a clean heart within you. This is His work; you cannot do it on your own, and you don't have to. God can take all that is wrong within you and make it right. The Good Shepherd can renew your soul and spirit; He restores you to the heavenly Father.

God will never withhold His mercy and grace from the one who confesses her sin and repents of it, putting her confidence and trust in the goodness of the Shepherd. Take time each day to bring your sins before God, trusting and believing He will remove them from you.

What thoughts plague you?

Discussion Question 59: Where do you need God's mercy and grace to overflow in your life today?

Just like the shepherd in Jesus' parable, the Good Shepherd pursues us relentlessly until we return to Him and abide with Him. How has Jesus pursued you in your life? Write about it here.

Day 5: The Shepherd's Voice

I am the good shepherd. I know My own and My own know Me, just as the Father knows Me and I know the Father; and I lay down My life for the sheep. And I have other sheep that are not of this fold. I must bring them also, and they will listen to My voice. So there will be one flock, one shepherd. For this reason the Father loves Me, because I lay down My life that I may take it up again. No one takes it from Me, but I lay it down of My own accord. I have authority to lay it down, and I have authority to take it up again. This charge I have received from My Father. (John 10:14–18)

Consider these points in this passage:

- Jesus is proclaiming for all to hear that He is the Good Shepherd.
- The Shepherd will lay down His life for His sheep on the cross, and He will take it up again (in His resurrection).
- Jesus knows you and loves you.
- The other sheep are the Gentiles.
- Jesus willingly stepped into this world to save His people.

Sheep know the voice of their shepherd. Each shepherd would have a chant or song he would sing to gather his flocks. It was easy for the sheep to stray away from the herd and become lost, but the sheep would listen to the voice of their shepherd to call them back to safety.

We hear the comforting voice of the Shepherd through God's Word.

What do you need to hear from the Good Shepherd today?

As I studied God as our Shepherd, I noticed a reference I had never seen before. I found it in Mark's retelling of feeding the five thousand. All four Gospels tell of this miracle. I combined details from all four accounts for this retelling. See Matthew 14:13–21; Mark 6:30–44; Luke 9:10–17; John 6:1–15.

The disciples were devastated; John the Baptist had been beheaded by Herod. They needed to find a quiet place to rest and spend time with Jesus, so He told them to "come away by yourselves to a desolate place and rest a while" (Mark 6:31). But there was little rest for them.

The people loved being around Jesus, and so they hurried to the other side of the Sea of Galilee when they saw the boat heading across. Soon there was a large crowd of about five thousand men, as well as women and children, waiting to hear Jesus teach and preach.

> When He went ashore He saw a great crowd, and He had compassion on them, because they were like sheep without a shepherd. And He began to teach them many things. (Mark 6:34)

Jesus chose to teach the people all day instead of resting. He was filled with compassion for them, and He created a place for them to hear His Word—His teaching. When evening came, the apostles began to wonder what all these people were going to eat. They were far away from any towns. They wondered if Jesus should stop preaching so the people could walk to a town and buy some food. Jesus knew the disciples were troubled. He asked one of them, "Philip, where can we buy bread for all of these people?"

Philip was from Bethsaida, a nearby town, and he knew it would cost a lot to buy food for over five thousand people. Philip answered Jesus, "I would have to work for at least six months to earn enough money to feed these people!"

Andrew, Simon Peter's brother, had been asking people in the crowd if they had any food. He found one boy with five barley loaves and two fish. Barley loaves were inexpensive and would have been about one inch thick and up to twenty inches in diameter. The fish were probably dried and salted and maybe the size of sardines.

Jesus said, "Divide all of the people into groups of fifty, and tell them to sit down on the grass." Soon, the whole crowd was divided into small groups.

And taking the five loaves and the two fish, He looked up
to heaven and said a blessing and broke the loaves and
gave them to the disciples to set before the people. And He
divided the two fish among them all. And they all ate and
were satisfied. And they took up twelve baskets full of broken
pieces and of the fish. (Mark 6:41–43)

Imagine what it would have been like to be one of the disciples and to
watch this scene unfold!

Discussion Question 60: In what other stories in Scripture do we see
God feeding His people? (Hint: It's in the Old Testament, in Exodus 16.)

Discussion Question 61: How does the story of Jesus feeding the people correlate with Psalm 23?

As we wrap up our study of God as our Shepherd, let's reflect on the
words of the hymn "The King of Love My Shepherd Is":

The King of love my shepherd is,
Whose goodness faileth never;
I nothing lack if I am His,
And He is mine forever.

Your Shepherd's goodness will never fail you. Even if everything else
falls apart, His promise to you cannot be broken. You can live a life of fullness in Him.

Where streams of living water flow,
My ransomed soul He leadeth
And, where the verdant pastures grow,
With food celestial feedeth.

The precious blood of Jesus has ransomed you. You are a treasure to
Him.

Perverse and foolish oft I strayed,
But yet in love He sought me
And on His shoulder gently laid
And home rejoicing brought me.

Keep the image of the Good Shepherd in your mind, and carry it with you through your life. Visualize how closely He holds you and how He looks at you. He loves you beyond measure.

What do you need to tell Him at this moment?

> In death's dark vale I fear no ill
> With thee, dear Lord, beside me,
> Thy rod and staff my comfort still,
> Thy cross before to guide me.

This world is broken and scary, and it's hard not to feel afraid sometimes. But remember, your Shepherd will lead you through the valley. You do not face it alone.

> Thou spreadst a table in my sight;
> Thine unction grace bestoweth;
> And, oh, what transport of delight
> From Thy pure chalice floweth!

Friend, I encourage you to partake of the Lord's Supper as often as it is offered. The gifts He gives to you in the Holy Supper are there to strengthen your faith and sustain you in your vocations.

> And so through all the length of days
> Thy goodness faileth never;
> Good Shepherd, may I sing Thy praise
> Within thy house forever![16]

You can sing praise to your Shepherd now and into eternity. May you rest in His goodness and love all through the length of your days.

In your journal time today, turn away from the storms of this life that threaten to separate you from the Lord, and lean into His promises and peace for you.

Week 7 Group Study Questions

Yahweh Ra'ah

Yahweh Ra'ah: *The Lord is my Shepherd*

Pronunciation: *Ya-way raw-aw'*

This name of God is based on Psalm 23 and adapted from a Hebrew verb, ro'iy, meaning "to shepherd." It calls to mind the One who faithfully provides for His flock and who meets their every need. Jesus called Himself our Good Shepherd, who watches over us constantly, protects from danger, and leads us to shelter in His presence. He is intimate with His people. In other words, He is a friend.

Bible Verse: *"The LORD is my shepherd; I shall not want." (Psalm 23:1)*

REFLECTIONS

- What stories stood out to you the most from this week's sessions? Why?
- What did you learn about God as Yahweh Ra'ah?

DISCUSSION QUESTIONS

55. How does knowing that the Good Shepherd is present for your every heartbeat make a difference in your day?

56. Where in your life do you need the peace of Jesus today?

57. How does knowing that the Good Shepherd walks with you through the valley of the shadow of death bring you comfort?

58. Where do you see the blessings from God overflowing in your life?

59. Where do you need God's mercy and grace to overflow in your life today?

60. In what other stories in Scripture do we see God feeding His people? (Hint: It's in the Old Testament, in Exodus 16.)

61. How does the story of Jesus feeding the people correlate with Psalm 23?

BENEDICTION

The LORD bless you and keep you;
The LORD make His face to shine upon you and be gracious to you;
The LORD lift up His countenance upon you and give you peace. (Numbers 6:24–26)

IMMANUEL

Immanuel: *God with us*

Pronunciation: ʿimmānûʾēl

Used twice in Isaiah and once in Matthew, the word Immanuel *means "God with us." Jesus is fully human and fully God, in what we describe as the two natures of Christ. He is the actual and true incarnation. Immanuel is a description of who Jesus is—God who has humbled Himself to be human among us. We can be assured that God is with us, will never leave us or forsake us, will bring us peace, and will keep His promises to us.*

Memory Verse: *"And the Word became flesh and dwelt among us, and we have seen His glory, glory as of the only Son from the Father, full of grace and truth." (John 1:14)*

Day 1: God with Us

Steam from my coffee cup carried the scent of mocha and mint through the air in our sunroom as I contemplated my plans for the day. That is, until the sound of a broken heart pierced the silence of the morning. My youngest son crashed through the front door. "Mom! Tiger Lily has been hit by a car! I saw the whole thing. I couldn't stop her."

My heart splintered as I thought about my son watching our beloved cat die.

Tiger Lily had adopted us when she was a tiny kitten. We created a home for her on our back patio, and she quickly became a family pet. But she didn't live in the house with us because of my allergies.

Tiger Lily allowed us to have a front-row seat for the birth of her kittens. We marveled at how God created her to know how to care for her babies. She would wait for me to come and talk to her by our back patio door each morning. Tiger Lily was dependent on me to care for her.

Thoughts of her life ending under the wheels of a car swirled in a torrent—poor kitty! Poor son who saw it! Poor me, who had to deal with her broken body! God help me—I couldn't leave her out there until Troy got home from work. So, blinded by tears, I grabbed an old towel and trudged to the side of the road where she lay.

Choking back the tears, I gently picked up her limp little body—our sweet and sassy cat was gone. I wailed as I carried Tiger Lily to her home on our patio. Because of the heat of the summer day, we buried her right away. Jacob dug the hole, and I wrapped her in the towel. Then, grief commingling with the melody of birds up in the trees, we said our goodbyes to the cat who had captured our hearts.

I had told my husband on multiple occasions that he would need to manage the situation if something ever happened to one of our pets. I was certain I would not be able to handle it. But the day Tiger Lily died, I was the one to do the job. It was hard, and we were so sad, but God gave me resolve for the task.

Perhaps you are like me and are ensnared by worried thinking. Do you feel trapped and weighed down by thoughts too heavy to carry? When we dwell on the drama that comes from spinning anxious stories out of proportion, the distress we feel can become a prison.

We place our infinite God within our finite limits.

Trying to control every aspect of life leaves us exhausted and weary. We think we can keep bad things from happening, but life doesn't work that way. God assures us, through His Word, that we never have to face our worst fears or grief alone. He dwells with us; we rest in the shadow of His wings.

The death of a pet is difficult and sad and something we would rather not face. It's a bad thing we cannot keep from happening. We cannot prevent or avoid the death of our loved ones either.

While I was working on this study, Troy became ill and ended up in the critical care unit at the hospital because of low sodium. The week before this happened, I had prepared for a women's retreat based on the theme of how Jesus is our rock and how we can rest in His unshakable faithfulness. I had spent hours studying God's Word and preparing to encourage the women at the retreat with the promises of our Immanuel. It was a lesson I put to use much sooner than I could have expected.

Those same promises sustained me through a long week. Jesus, our Immanuel, was with my husband as the medical team helped bring healing to his body. God's Word was a comfort to my wearied heart and his.

Often, our worries come from not being able to control a situation. The truth is that we cannot plan for all the uncertainties we will face, but we can trust our Immanuel, the God who is with us, to give us His strength and His peace through all the trials and troubles we will face in this life.

Discussion Question 62: What fears do you have about what might happen in the future?

Take some time to think and write. Ask God to meet you in your fearful state and to surround you with His peace.

Uncertainties of life are inevitable. The things of this world are temporary. But Immanuel, God with us, is our refuge and strength here and now. We see His promise of Immanuel first in Isaiah 7:14: "Therefore the Lord Himself will give you a sign. Behold, the virgin shall conceive and bear a son, and shall call His name Immanuel." We see this promise fulfilled in Matthew:

> "She will bear a son, and you shall call His name Jesus, for He will save His people from their sins." All this took place to fulfill what the Lord had spoken by the prophet: "Behold, the virgin shall conceive and bear a son, and they shall call His name Immanuel" (which means, God with us). (Matthew 1:21–23)

We started this study in Genesis, and we will end with the reference to Genesis found in the first chapter of John.

> In the beginning was the Word, and the Word was with God, and the Word was God. He was in the beginning with God. All things were made through Him, and without Him was not any thing made that was made. In Him was life, and the life was the light of men. The light shines in the darkness, and the darkness has not overcome it. . . . And the Word became flesh and dwelt among us, and we have seen His glory, glory as of the only Son from the Father, full of grace and truth. (John 1:1–5, 14)

Jesus is entirely God and fully human. He is the One who spoke the universe into existence. He is the Word who became flesh to dwell among us.

The King of all creation humbled Himself to enter this world as a human. The One who designed us in our mother's womb was formed the same way in His mother, Mary. He went through the same human process of fetal development that we did.

God chose to put His Son in the care of two faithful peasants. In the fullness of time, God planned precisely the time and place Jesus would be born. Do you ever wonder why God orchestrated the event to unfold the way it did?

From my human perspective, when I consider creation in all its glory, I am amazed that God didn't choose a majestic setting in which the King of kings would be born, instead of in a feeding trough in a smelly, dirty stable. When I think of all of the other names of Jesus in the Bible—Wonderful Counselor, Mighty God, Everlasting Father, Prince of Peace, Lord of all, great High Priest, Son of the Highest—my impulse would be to put baby Jesus in a lush valley or a beautiful garden. But God's choice of when and where to place Immanuel shows that He came for everyone. God coming to earth in such a humble state communicates His choice to be a real person with real people. He is our Immanuel, God with us, even in the most wretched of conditions.

The angels didn't announce the birth of Jesus to royalty or the religious elite; they shared the news with shepherds. We romanticize the shepherds, but their lives were difficult, and they were often considered the bottom rung of society. They were quite rough around the edges, yet God revealed the Savior of the world to them first. The ones who watched over the Passover lambs were the first to worship the Lamb of God.

Jesus came for everyone. He stepped into the brokenness of this world to bring His light into the darkness. Our omnipotent God humbled Himself to become an infant, dependent upon human parents to feed Him and change His diapers.

The angels could not hold back their joy, the shepherds could not bridle their worship, and God did not hesitate to offer His grace and mercy for you and me.

In what ways do you need to be reminded that God is with you? Here are some suggestions, but you may identify other ways unique to you.

- Your thought life
- Family joys and sorrows
- Health
- Work
- Raising children in a culture that hates God
- Aging parents
- Launching your young adult children into the world

Take time to think about this. Pay attention to your thoughts throughout your day to see where you may have forgotten that He is with you. Your Immanuel is Lord over all your life. In the peace of His presence, ask Him for help. He is with you.

SCRIPTURE PRAYER

On the day I called, You answered me; my strength of soul
You increased. (Psalm 138:3)

BENEDICTION

The LORD bless you and keep you;
The LORD make His face to shine upon you and be gracious
to you;
The LORD lift up His countenance upon you and give you
peace. (Numbers 6:24–26)

When we set expectations or standards for others, we limit them and set ourselves up for disappointment. Trust the Holy Spirit to remove the limits set by your expectations and continuously expand your faith in God's wisdom and power.

Day 2: Remember the Promises

When we remember that God is with us, our life changes. The day my husband was rushed to the hospital, the day my dad suffered a heart attack, the day I learned my grandmother was dying of cancer—on each of these days, my faith in my Savior strengthened me to face what, to me, felt impossible. I can see how Immanuel provided a shelter of peace for me then, and He promises to continue.

Psalm 91 talks about being in the shelter of God's wings. He is a resting place where we can be protected. Like a mother bird with her babies safe under her wings, God shelters us.

Our lives might be falling apart, but when we are in the arms of Immanuel, who loves us and promises never to leave our side, we find rest.

God provides this for us. His provision rivals nothing we can create on our own. Jesus tells us we can abide in Him. He offers us His peace.

> But the Helper, the Holy Spirit, whom the Father will send in My name, He will teach you all things and bring to your remembrance all that I have said to you. Peace I leave with you; My peace I give to you. Not as the world gives do I give to you. Let not your hearts be troubled, neither let them be afraid. (John 14:26–27)

In this passage, Jesus was talking to His disciples, preparing them for what is about to come. Jesus knew He would die on the cross the next day. His words of comfort and peace to the disciples are also for all of us, forever.

When Jesus offers you His peace, it comes directly from Him. It's a truly lasting peace. Jesus also tells us He will send the Holy Spirit to help us remember all He has taught us.

What challenges or uncertainties are you facing in your life? Take an inventory of what you spend most of your time trying to figure out. Where do you give most of your time and energy? This might take you a while to think through; that is okay. Don't rush through this process, because it is important.

Here's my list (you can use mine or create your own):

- Aging parents and in-laws
- Learning to let go of my adult children
- Getting older
- Anxious thoughts leftover from COVID and how to move forward

Discussion Question 63: Pick one of these or one from your own list to examine in the light of God's peace.

I am reminded of a time when my family's whole world changed overnight and how Immanuel helped us.

Our boys attended a small Christian school for several years. It felt like home to us, and our boys loved being there. But the school faced significant financial challenges. There were many ideas for solving the problem, and as a school board member, I had a front-row seat to what was going on. I was devastated over decisions made by a small group of people that I thought were harmful to school families and that conflicted with what the school stood for.

Over time, Troy and I found the situation unbearable. We made the gut-wrenching decision to pull our boys out of the school and enroll them elsewhere. The night before their final day at the school we loved so much, I lay awake, wondering if we were making the right decision. Would our boys be okay? Would we mess up their lives forever?

The last day I drove them to that school was Grandparents' Day. The boys were so excited, because their grandparents would be there. They had no idea it would be their last day at that school. It broke my heart not to share the reason for our decision, but they were too young to understand. We didn't want to burden them with an adult decision.

After I dropped them off, I planned to check out another Christian school, but I could not pull myself together to do it. I drove around in a daze, then went home and poured my heart out to God with snot-filled sobs.

When Troy's parents brought them home from school, we explained our decision to the boys. Their grief shattered my heart, and I questioned every decision I had ever made as a parent. We held them close and let them cry, our tears merging with theirs.

When we told the boys about the new school we wanted to check out, they surprised us by saying, "We want to be homeschooled." Troy and I understood their hearts—they didn't want to walk into a new school in November.

God took the broken pieces of our hearts and mended them back together. He poured out His blessings upon our family. As their homeschool teacher, I spent hours talking with our boys and learning alongside them. Even though that year brought a lot of grief for our family, it also provided some of my most treasured memories as a mom. Our sons loved homeschooling so much that we continued through high school.

Sharing this story with you reminds me that God helped our family transition through a hard time and that He will help us in the future.

What stories do you need to remember?

How has God been your shelter in the past?

How do you need Immanuel to help you in your life today?

Recall the gifts of your Baptism, and rejoice that your sins are washed away by water and the Word to give you new life in Christ Jesus.

Day 3: You Never Cry Alone

When I was a director of Christian education, I worked with many young people and their parents. One of my greatest joys was to teach confirmation class, culminating with the students professing their faith on their confirmation day. In some churches, the students would write and share a statement of faith. I loved to hear each student share their beliefs.

I will never forget one statement of faith that touched my heart deeply. I think it will impact you too.

She walked to the front of the church with fear written across her face and her knees shaking. She stood there for a moment, gathering her composure as tears slipped quietly down her face. Then her dad walked down the aisle, hugged her, and stood at her side with his arm around her.

She spoke: "My favorite Bible verse is, 'Jesus wept' [John 11:35]. And it's not because it's the shortest verse in the Bible." The congregation chuckled softly. "I love it because it reminds me that Jesus understands my tears, and I never cry alone."

There wasn't a dry eye in the church. Her simple and profound childlike faith touched our souls and encouraged our hearts. That young woman reminded me that each tear I shed does not go unnoticed by Immanuel.

READ JOHN 11:17—44

Have you stood in the valley of the shadow of death? Have you had a close call that made you realize how tenuous life can be? Have you ever been overwhelmed by devices that kept a loved one's lungs working and heart pumping? Perhaps you've watched helplessly as sickness consumed the life of a relative, or perhaps you have lingered graveside, gazing in disbelief, wondering how life can end so abruptly.

Each of us eventually becomes familiar with the valley of the shadow of death. After experiences such as these, we see life from a different perspective. Perhaps you are in the valley right now. If so, may the words of our Immanuel bring you peace and comfort.

In the passage from John 11, Martha is filled with grief, and we can hear the sorrow in her words. "If only You had been here" (see v. 21). She stares into the face of Jesus with heartache in her eyes. Her brother is dead, and the One who could have changed everything hadn't even been there for the funeral.

You need our Immanuel especially in such times as these, because only He can stand in the valley of the shadow of death and offer comfort, hope, and answers.

Listen to what Jesus tells Martha, because those words are meant for all of us to hear.

> Jesus said to her, "I am the resurrection and the life. Whoever believes in Me, though he dies, yet shall he live, and everyone who lives and believes in Me shall never die. Do you believe this?" She said to Him, "Yes, Lord; I believe that You are the Christ, the Son of God, who is coming into the world." (John 11:25–27)

Jesus asks you too: "Do you believe this?" What is your answer? Notice that Martha's answer is a loud and strong confession of faith. But moments later, when Jesus asks for the stone to be rolled away, she has doubts. The stink of death has settled in, and she is wondering what Jesus could do for Lazarus now.

Does Jesus change His mind because her faith wavered? No, He doesn't change. We can find great comfort in this, because we also have times when our faith is strong but we experience doubts at the same time.

We are not defined by a moment of weakness, because faith is not dependent upon our feelings. Faith is a gift from God, given freely and refreshed daily. He knows our trust will rise and fall through uncertainties, but He does not change; His promises hold fast.

You will weep over the deaths of family and friends. Remember that Immanuel grieves and cries with you. As you mourn, rely on His promise that death does not have the final say over your loved one. Your Savior won the victory over sin, death, and the devil. He defeated death and gives us eternal life with Him. And on that Last Day, Jesus will call us all forth from our graves, and we will join Him in the place He has prepared for us.

If you were asked to give a statement of faith, what would it be?

> **Discussion Question 64:** Death is a part of our life. How can Immanuel provide His peace for you today?

The Lord sees your every flaw and every sin, yet He loves you so much that He sent Jesus to be your Redeemer and Savior. Thank Him today for His forgiveness and love!

Day 4: When You Feel Weary

As I write this during the second summer of the pandemic, everyday life is starting to feel more normal. That said, weariness still weighs heavily upon my heart. The world has endured an emotional toll from the challenges of this crisis, and even when the worst is behind us, the impact will be felt throughout our lives.

Here's an example: during that time, I developed a summer cold. It had all the signs and symptoms of a cold; unfortunately for me, it settled into my lungs, and I have asthma. My niece was getting married, and I had been looking forward to the event for a long time. Before COVID, a summer cold was a summer cold—no big deal. Now, if I go anywhere with a cough, people duck, step away, and give me "The Look." (I am not judging because I have the same reactions. I wish I didn't, but I do.) My cough was due to my asthma, but I couldn't wear a big sign explaining that.

I chose to go to the wedding ceremony but not to the reception. As I sat home that evening, I thought about all the things we missed out on because of the pandemic, and I felt weary and sad.

We all suffered losses in those months. It isn't helpful when we consider one loss to be more significant than another, because a loss of any magnitude generates emotions that are personal and significant for each individual.

The following strategies helped me as I worked through the grief of 2020 and beyond. Perhaps these suggestions will help you too:

- Notice and name your feelings or emotions. If you can journal or create a word picture of how you feel, that will help you move forward.
- Talk to a trusted family member, friend, mentor, or pastor.

- Don't be afraid to talk to a counselor. He or she can give you the tools and resources you need.
- Join or start a small-group Bible study. We did this at our church with a group of women, and we found spending time in God's Word with other women helped us all.
- Sit in the presence of God. Pour out your heart before Him. This is an ongoing process. God does not grow disheartened by listening to you or helping you.

You may feel emotionally frayed because you don't always get to choose the stories that become a part of your life, but be assured that God writes your story. Immanuel holds you close to His heart. He gives you His Word to strengthen and remind you of the hope you have in Him.

> Come to Me, all who labor and are heavy laden, and I will give you rest. Take My yoke upon you, and learn from Me, for I am gentle and lowly in heart, and you will find rest for your souls. For My yoke is easy, and My burden is light. (Matthew 11:28–30)

The verb *come* is in the present tense. Jesus invites you to come right now. Set aside your burdens, your anxious thoughts, and your troubles. He asks to you come to Him, to be in His presence.

Notice what He offers: "I will give you rest" (v. 28). This is a gift of His grace toward you. You don't need to earn it in three simple steps. The word for *rest* is also in the present tense, meaning it is available to you immediately. He promises full and complete rest in Him right now.

Jesus invites you to set aside the burden you are carrying. Is it the yoke of your sin, the sins committed against you, or the weight of listening to Satan's lies about who you are? The devil wants you to think that you are not enough and that your sins are too grievous for Jesus to forgive. He wants you to believe you need to earn your salvation, to earn forgiveness, and to earn God's love. It is not possible to achieve these things on our own, but the good news is we don't need to, because Christ has already secured them for us.

The yoke Jesus is talking about in verse 29 is the one He gives to you. It is lined with His love and His grace. He will show you the way of grace. Your salvation and forgiveness of sins are completed in Him. The burden is light because we are yoked with Jesus, and He pulls the weight for us.

Jesus again promises that we can find rest for our souls in Him. Our most immense burden was sin, but Jesus has taken care of that for us. We all walk through the sinful world and the sorrow it brings, and as we do, Jesus, our Immanuel, walks with us. He carries our burdens and sorrows with Him. He invites us to learn from Him by spending time in His Word, reading it, and hearing His Gospel message preached.

Discussion Question 65: What burden or sorrow have you been trying to carry on your own?

A few years ago, I visited the volcanoes on the Big Island of Hawaii. There had been recent volcanic activity in the past few years, and I noticed vibrant and beautiful flowers growing up from the ashes. All around me were lovely plants growing strong and green amidst the destruction. It took my breath away. We are all like those flowers.

Life, with its uncertainties, is like a volcano. We don't know when it will erupt, but when it does, it changes everything—the landscape is never the same. But Immanuel stands with us and helps us flourish in the aftermath of destruction. We might need to reimagine what life will look like, but we can take comfort knowing Jesus is with us now and on the other side. Immanuel offers His hope and comfort, and in that, there is beauty.

Where in your life do you need to be reminded of Immanuel's hope and comfort?

I love the prayer in Ephesians 3:14–21. Read the words slowly and let them settle into your soul.

> For this reason I bow my knees before the Father, from
> whom every family in heaven and on earth is named, that
> according to the riches of His glory He may grant you to be
> strengthened with power through His Spirit in your inner
> being, so that Christ may dwell in your hearts through

faith—that you, being rooted and grounded in love, may have strength to comprehend with all the saints what is the breadth and length and height and depth, and to know the love of Christ that surpasses knowledge, that you may be filled with all the fullness of God.

Now to Him who is able to do far more abundantly than all that we ask or think, according to the power at work within us, to Him be glory in the church and in Christ Jesus throughout all generations, forever and ever. Amen.

May God strengthen your heart and your soul as you meditate on these verses. Immanuel's love for you covers everything. Rest in His love. Know that you are held in His capable hands.

Think about hymns that are sung at funerals, and reflect on how they point the hearers to the peace we have in knowing that our salvation in Jesus is certain.

Day 5: Come and Receive the Gifts of Grace

Sweat trickled down my back as the hot steam rose from the scalding hot dishwater. Salty tears left tracks on my face.

Hot and miserable thoughts swirled through my mind. I had managed to fight with all three of my siblings that day. It started as typical sibling squabbles over silly things, but it turned ugly. I let my temper grab hold of my tongue, and now that my anger had subsided, I was deeply ashamed of what I had said. I learned I could not take my actions and words back. I apologized, but the stench would linger for a while. I had even yelled at my mom, and that was the final straw. My punishment was to wash and dry all the supper dishes by myself.

The humidity was so high that day in northern Minnesota that everything felt damp and sticky. We didn't have air conditioning because most summer days were delightful. Such high humidity was rare.

I longed for a breeze to stir the curtains at the kitchen window, but the air was still. There was a fuchsia plant hanging in front of the window. It was covered with brilliant pink and purple flowers. Their beauty caught my attention.

I poured out my heart before God, asking Him to forgive me. I didn't understand how He could or even why Jesus would want to, after the way I had acted that day.

I hung my head in shame and repented of my sins. It was painful to think of them all, but I handed them over.

A whirring noise filled the air. I looked up. Right in front of the window was a hummingbird. It hovered and seemed to look right at me. Delight tickled my heart, and I felt a smile tug at my mouth for the first time that day. The little bird squeaked and chirped at me for a few moments. I was captivated by the tiny creature; I had never heard one make those noises before.

In those moments, I knew God's peace. The little bird captured my attention, and I remembered how much God loves me. My sin was great, but His love for me was greater. Jesus' words about worry in Matthew 6:25–34 came to mind. If God cares for even the hummingbirds and the flowers on the fuchsia, then He cares about me as well. The lesson in that passage is about God's provision of food and clothing. What God provides that we need even more than these basics is forgiveness and the promise of eternity with Him.

Our greatest struggles revolve around our sins and the sins against us. We live in a broken and fallen world. Yet Jesus defeated sin, and it will not have the final say over us. Immanuel stepped into the darkness to give us the light of His grace and mercy.

READ JOHN 21

Notice how Jesus treats the disciples in this chapter. It's important to note this is the third time Jesus has seen His disciples since He rose from the grave. We know only the details John writes for us, and we need to remember God instructed him in his writings.

We begin as Peter and the disciples were fishing. I always wonder why they were fishing. Did they think Jesus was finished with them, so they just went back to their regular jobs? Jesus called them to be His disciples, and He hadn't demoted them. We place our thoughts and actions upon God, thinking He will handle situations the same way we do.

The disciples spent all night fishing and didn't catch anything. Jesus stood on the shore and called out to them, inquiring if they had caught any fish, but they did not recognize Him.

They told Him they hadn't caught any fish, and Jesus directed them to throw the net on the right side of the boat because there were fish there. They cast the net, and it became so full they could not haul it in.

John said to Peter, "It is the Lord!" (v. 7). Then Peter, in all his exuberance, jumped into the water and swam to shore. He could not wait for the boat; Peter wanted to get to Jesus right away.

Jesus said, "Come and have breakfast" (v. 12). I love this part of the story, because the disciples knew what they had done. Just a few days prior, they had abandoned Jesus in the Garden of Gethsemane. The only disciple who was at the trials and crucifixion was John, yet the resurrected Jesus had appeared to the disciples on two other occasions. Never once did He remind them of their failures.

I don't know about you, but when someone fails to do something for me, I tell them. And when I've failed others, they let me know too. But Jesus didn't count their sins against them. Instead, we see this beautiful picture of grace and mercy. The King of all creation, whom God raised from the dead, invited His disciples to breakfast, and He served them.

Think about someone who has betrayed or abandoned you; would you want to serve them breakfast? If you had betrayed someone and they wanted to serve you breakfast, how would you feel?

Here we see Immanuel's love for His friends. This scene reminds me of the table God prepares for us as we receive the Lord's Supper. Every time it is offered, Jesus gives us His body and blood in the bread and the wine. It is there, friends, that we receive a precious gift. It doesn't matter what kind of week we've had, whether it's been terrific or horrific, or even one so filled with sin we are not sure if we should even step foot into the church. Regardless, Jesus invites us to come before the Table and receive the feast He has prepared for us.

In our own preparation for this precious gift, it's essential to examine our hearts and confess our sins. How else are we to know how much we need it? You see, friends, when we confess our sins, Jesus takes them away from us. What happens when we gather at the table?

- He gives us grace.
- He gives us forgiveness.
- He gives us the strength to face the following week.
- Oh, He gives lovely gifts.

He says, "Come, come to the table; come, all of you, no matter what kind of week you have had; come to the table and receive."

Discussion Question 66: What questions do you have about Holy Communion? How do you prepare yourself for the Lord's Supper?

Later in the passage, Jesus had a conversation with Peter. Now, this portion of Scripture is often a source of discussion. Jesus asked Peter three times if Peter loved Him. Some people believe Jesus asked him three times because that is how many times Peter denied Him; however, if you can read the text in Greek, you'll notice something interesting.

The Greek language has different words for love, which makes sense. The love you have for your friends is different from the love you would have for your spouse or children. When Jesus starts talking to Peter about love, He uses the word *agape*, which means "unconditional love." It's the perfect love God has for us. There are no conditions placed on that love. The kind of love Peter is talking about is *phileo*, which is the friendship kind of love. You are fond of the person, but it's not the same as agape love. Consider this retelling of the story using the words for love used by Jesus and Peter:

> When breakfast was over, Jesus drew Peter aside and said, "Peter do you agape Me?" Peter responded, "Yes, Lord, You know I phileo You."
>
> Jesus said to him, "Feed My lambs." A second time, Jesus said, "Peter, do you agape Me?" Peter replied, "Yes, Lord; You know I phileo You." Jesus told him, "Tend My sheep."
>
> Then Jesus asked him a third time, using the word for love that Peter used. "Peter, do you phileo Me?" Peter was sad that Jesus asked him a third time if he loved Him. And Peter responded, "Lord, You know everything; You know I phileo You." Jesus replied, "Feed My sheep."

Imagine the scene. Peter, the one who denied Jesus three times, has been restored, and Jesus is asking Peter to take care of the Church. He is entrusting it to Peter.

How do you think Peter felt about leading the Church? What roles do you serve in your church? What comfort can you receive from this story as you go about serving?

As we think about this event, we know that even in our most difficult moments, when we turn our back on God, forget about His love for us, or don't love Jesus as best as we can, Immanuel looks at us and says, "I agape you. My love for you is not based on what you do. It's based upon who I am."

The next time you receive the Lord's Supper, think about the gift of grace you are receiving. Rest in the perfect love of your Immanuel.

Someday, if Jesus doesn't come back first, you will breathe your final breath here on earth and close your eyes. When you open your eyes again, you will see your Immanuel—the Word made flesh. He will welcome you home and invite you to come and feast at the banquet that will last forever.

> On this mountain the LORD of hosts will make for all peoples
> a feast of rich food, a feast of well-aged wine, of rich food full
> of marrow, of aged wine well refined. And He will swallow
> up on this mountain the covering that is cast over all peoples,
> the veil that is spread over all nations. He will swallow up
> death forever; and the Lord GOD will wipe away tears from
> all faces, and the reproach of His people He will take away
> from all the earth, for the LORD has spoken. (Isaiah 25:6–8)

But until that day comes, you can rest in the promises of Immanuel—the God who chooses you and gives you the peace of His presence, now and for all eternity.

Describe your journey from lack of rest to rest, from anxious thoughts to peace, that this study has provided you. Remember that Immanuel is with you in every storm and is your refuge and source of hope, today and for eternity.

WEEK 8 GROUP STUDY QUESTIONS

IMMANUEL

Immanuel: *God with us*

Pronunciation: ʿ*immānûʾēl*

Used twice in Isaiah and once in Matthew, the word Immanuel *means "God with us." Jesus is fully human and fully God, in what we describe as the two natures of Christ. He is the actual and true incarnation. Immanuel is a description of who Jesus is—God who has humbled Himself to be human among us. We can be assured that God is with us, will never leave us or forsake us, will bring us peace, and will keep His promises to us.*

Memory Verse: *"And the Word became flesh and dwelt among us, and we have seen His glory, glory as of the only Son from the Father, full of grace and truth." (John 1:14)*

REFLECTIONS

- What stories stood out to you the most from this week's lessons? Why?
- What did you learn about God as Immanuel?

DISCUSSION QUESTIONS

62. What fears do you have about what might happen in the future?

63. Pick one of these or one from your own list (see page 200) to examine in the light of God's peace.

64. Death is a part of our life. How can Immanuel provide His peace for you today?

65. What burden or sorrow have you been trying to carry on your own?

66. What questions do you have about Holy Communion? How do you prepare yourself for the Lord's Supper?

BENEDICTION

The LORD bless you and keep you;
The LORD make His face to shine upon you and be gracious to you;
The LORD lift up His countenance upon you and give you peace. (Numbers 6:24–26)

Acknowledgments

God, thank You for holding me in Your capable hands, close to Your heart, and surrounding me with Your peace.

Troy, words cannot express how thankful I am for your love and support through this process. Through the joy and sorrows of life, God has brought us all within the peace of His presence.

Jacob and Matthew, thank you for listening and helping me through the writing of this book.

Mom and Dad, I love you. Thank you for believing in me and being my biggest cheerleaders in all things.

Jimella, Sheila, and David, my fondest memories from childhood include the three of you. I love you all very much.

St. Paul Lutheran Church and ACT, thank you for being an important part of my growing-up years and for all the love and support you have given to me.

Pastor Eric Obermann, thank you for reading my study and giving me feedback.

Women of Grace Bible study, thank you for your prayers and cheering me on.

Rachael, Shannon, and Angie, thank you for being a part of my think-tank group. I will always cherish the memory of us sitting around my kitchen table.

Cheryl, thank you for all your help with my book proposal. Your writing expertise has helped me many times throughout the years, and I am grateful.

Sharla, thank you for your encouragement and extra eyes on my book proposal at the beginning of this journey; your kindness means so much to me.

Cherie, thank you for all our long conversations as I sorted through the writing process.

Stephenie, thank you for sharing your wisdom with me and giving me feedback.

Laura Lane, thank you for your willingness to listen to my idea and take a chance on a first-time author.

Peggy, thank you for being my editor and helping me through this process. I am grateful for you.

CPH team, thank you for everything. I am grateful for every single moment you have poured into helping make *Promised Rest* ready to go out into the world. It has been an honor to work with you.

Thank you to everyone who has prayed and encouraged me through this process; it has meant so much to me.

ANSWERS TO DISCUSSION QUESTIONS

WEEK 1

1. Answers will vary, but you can find comfort in knowing that Elohim calls you by name and that you belong to Him. Whatever trials you face, He promises to be with you.

2. Everyone's circumstances will be different, but knowing that God knows our names gives us peace.

3. Answers will vary but may include the following: situations you cannot control, the health and well-being of family and friends, the aftermath of the pandemic, finances, and so on.

4. Elohim shelters you in the peace of His presence, and you will never face trouble alone. Answers may vary, but the reminder is that God stands with us and strengthens us to face adversity.

5. Reflections will vary. We can apply the words of Isaiah 40:28–31 to our daily lives; whether our challenges are big or small, God gives us what we need to face the moment.

6. Answers will vary but might include the following: the walls around a castle, the security of the Pentagon or other buildings, a storm cellar, or a safe room in a basement.

7. Insights will vary, but knowing that God's love and promises to you will never change but remain constant and steady brings our hearts hope.

8. Answers will vary, but what are you grateful for today or this week? Is there a hymn or a song that puts into words what is stirring in your heart?

9. Answers will vary but may include times of family crises, uncertain moments, health concerns, and life challenges that catch us unprepared.

10. Again, answers will vary, but remembering how God helped the Israelites at the Red Sea brings comfort to our stories. When we cannot see a way out, we can rest in knowing God is with us, and we can trust in who He is.

WEEK 2

11. This a personal question, so participants will share according to how comfortable they are. Our earthly fathers impact how we see God, but the precious truth is that God's love for you is perfect.

12. Answers will vary, but it could be as simple as praying the Lord's Prayer, saying the Apostles' Creed, and slowing down as you pray it.

13. Answers will vary. Responses might include that it depends on the sin. We cannot hide our sins from God, and He wants us to come to Him. Abba meets us with love and covers us with His grace.

14. As you answer this question, think of how the father responded to both of his sons in the parable of the prodigal son. That is how God responds to you.

15. Answers will vary. We all are similar to both sons. Regardless, God the Father is full of mercy and grants us His forgiveness.

16. Answers will vary. God's grace covers every sin, and we don't need to hide in shame from Him.

17. Answers will vary. We may wonder if we are enough when we forget we are made in God's image and how much He loves us.

18. Every person will see this differently. We all deal with fear and grief differently. We have no control over anything, and we can rest in the presence of the One (Jesus) who controls all things.

19. Answers could include the Word, Sacrament, worship, and brothers and sisters in Christ.

20. Answers will vary. We live in a society that places priority on instant answers. We are not good at waiting. The longest the author can remember waiting for something is twenty years.

21. Answers will vary as women share from their own lives times when they have felt unseen. For many, it could be in relationships or on the job.

22. Answers might vary; some participants might not know, and that is okay. The Psalms are always a good place to start.

23. Answers will vary. For many, the pandemic will stand out as something we didn't choose, but we had to learn how to keep moving forward.

24. Answers might vary. When we don't trust God and take solutions into our own hands, things can get messy. We must learn to live with the consequences of our actions. God doesn't withhold His love and promises from us.

25. Each reader will respond to this question differently. When the author looks at the story from her viewpoint, she is surprised because she is basing it on how she would handle it. God is always full of tenderness and compassion toward His children.

26. The questions become more reflective as we go through the psalm. Some participants may say there are definitely details they wish they could hide from the Creator.

27. Answers will vary greatly.

28. Answers will vary greatly.

29. Answers will vary, but encourage participants to identify a verse or two.

WEEK 4

30. *Abide* means "to dwell or reside." *Abide* means "to rest in the presence of God."

31. *El Shaddai* means "all-sufficient"; we can trust Him to supply all our needs.

32. Answers will vary. If you know your baptismal date, share it with your group, or see if you can find it. God claimed you as His own dear child through the waters of Holy Baptism.

33. Waiting is hard, especially when the outcome seems impossible from our human perspective; all things are possible with God.

34. God extended to Isaac the promise He gave to Abraham. Ishmael was not the son of the promise, but God included him in His blessings and protection. God did not break His covenant with Abraham even though Abraham took matters into his own hands.

35. Knowing that God is sufficient for all we need removes worry and fear. Even when we forget that God knows our needs and provides for them, we need not worry because we are forgiven in Christ Jesus.

36. Answers will vary. Bitterness happens when we let anger take root in our hearts, and it grows. Forgiveness, asking for God's help, and Christian counseling can help you deal with bitterness.

37. Forgiveness is hard. El Shaddai's grace meets us where we are and helps us forgive what may feel unforgivable.

38. Daily, we need God's grace and peace to multiply in our lives with our relationships, our church families, our communities, our nation, and our world.

39. Answers will vary.

WEEK 5

40. Answers will vary. God provides the peace of His presence for us in all situations.

41. Answers will vary. Possible questions include the following: What was their conversation? How did Isaac feel? Did he believe that God would work it out? Was he scared? What were Abraham's thoughts? There are so many different questions we could ask.

42. As I look at this story, I see the details only God could arrange: Moses was protected by Pharaoh because of his daughter; Jochebed was able to care for Moses in safety; when Jochebed placed Moses into God's hands, God gave him back to her in the most unexpected way.

43. Answers may relate to family, job security, finances, friendship, or work struggles. God holds us in His capable hands. Read Psalm 91 as a prayer for your loved ones.

44. Jesus would look at us with love and compassion. His grace toward us is far greater than any sin.

45. Trust God to do what He says He will do with your sins—remove them. If you feel shame, talk to a pastor or Christian counselor; he or she can help you work through it.

WEEK 6

46. What-if thinking impacts how we feel emotionally and physically, how we view life, and how we see people. Philippians 4:4–9 applies especially well here, as do Psalm 8, Psalm 9:9–10, and Psalm 91:9–16.

47. Spend time talking to God through praying out loud or through journaling. Answers will vary.

48. Money, people, or a false sense of being able to control circumstances. Answers will vary.

49. When bad things happen, we ask God why. It's not wrong to ask God questions, and I would like to think that if I could see God, I would have the same questions for Him. Answers will vary.

50. Answers will vary but will include topics such as parenting, health crises, living in a global pandemic, traveling, starting a new job, and so on.

51. God's patience and compassion are surprising when we view the story through how we would handle it. It's comforting to know that God does not turn away from us in anger over our fears.

52. Answers will vary. We look for peace where it cannot be found: people, money, job security, possessions, media, government, and the list goes on. True peace can only come from God, and He offers it to us. We don't need to earn it.

53. Because the Church is comprised of sinners, there are many reasons for it to be difficult and complicated for each of us.

54. Participants may respond with elements of the service that include confession, absolution and forgiveness, prayers, and hymns. God comes to us in worship through the Word and the Sacrament.

WEEK 7

55. Knowing that the Good Shepherd walks with us through each moment helps us face what feels impossible or uncertain.

56. Answers will vary. We need the peace of Jesus in every moment, and He gives it to us.

57. The Good Shepherd promised to be with us always. Jesus endured death on the cross for us and rose victorious from the grave so that we may have eternal life with Him.

58. Answers will vary. God's blessings overflow when we read His Word, attend the Divine Service, and receive the Lord's Supper. God's blessings flow through the love of family and friends.

59. God's grace and mercy need to overflow into every aspect of our life. Answers will vary but may include children, aging parents, employment challenges, health challenges, finances, and so on.

60. In one example, God provided manna and quail for the Israelites as they wandered in the desert.

61. The people needed to hear the words of Jesus, and they needed food; Jesus provided both. The Good Shepherd of Psalm 23 provides for all our needs.

WEEK 8

62. Answers will vary but will likely include concerns about loved ones, security, global issues, and so on. We cannot know the future, but we know the One who holds the future, and we can trust Him.

63. Answers will vary.

54. We can be comforted in remembering that death does not have the final say over our lives; God does. Answers will vary. This answer will change daily because of life circumstances.

65. We try to fix our problems on our own. Answers will vary, and this discussion could be more reflective. I didn't realize how much fear I was carrying because of the pandemic and the grief over all that was lost. May God help each one of us to remember we can bring everything to Him.

66. Answers will vary. The wonder of Holy Communion is that God would give us His body and blood to strengthen and offer forgiveness. Answers will vary on how each person prepares for communion, but answers should include a mention of self-examination regarding our sinfulness, our unworthiness to be forgiven, and our need for a Savior. The Divine Service prepares us to receive the gifts God gives us in the Lord's Supper.

NOTE FOR LEADERS ABOUT AN OPENING SESSION

Dear Leader,

One of the ways to quickly create community in a new Bible study group is an ice-breaker activity. To that end, I've created an opening for your first group meeting when you hand out books to the participants. You will see that I also have a small group activity listed below, but you can add this activity to any session.

Thank you for leading your group, and please know I am praying for you.

OPENING SESSION

Introductions: Have the participants introduce themselves and share a fun fact about themselves.

Read and review the introductory material on pages 00 to 00 with the group.

Discuss the journaling section with the group members. Share with them that they can design this study to fit their lives. It's okay if they don't have time to journal every day.

Mixer: In preparation for studying the name *Elohim* have the group talk about the most beautiful sight they have ever seen. If there is time, they can share more than one.

Group activity:

Note: The group leader should prepare for this activity by bringing smooth stones, such as those used in landscaping. The stones should be about the size of a tablespoon; large enough to write on.

Stones of Remembrance

In Joshua 4, we see God's people crossing the Jordan River into the Promised Land. God parts the water for His people so they can walk across. Here God commands His people to build altars with stones to help them remember what God has done. There is an altar in the middle of the Jordan River and there is also one at Gilgal.

You won't build an altar, but I encourage you to keep a stone of remembrance. I have brought some stones and some markers. On your stone, write the words, "Be still." Think of a place where you can keep this stone as a reminder of who God is and that you are His beloved child.

Benediction.

> The LORD bless you and keep you;
> The LORD make His face to shine upon you and be gracious to you;
> The LORD lift up His countenance upon you and give you peace.
> (Numbers 6:24-26)

ENDNOTES

1 *Luther's Works*, American Edition, vol. 56, edited by Benjamin T. G. Mayes (St. Louis, MO: Concordia Publishing House, 2018), 237–38.

2 Adapted from *Luther's Small Catechism with Explanation* (St. Louis, MO: Concordia Publishing House, 1986, 2017), 19–20.

3 *Lutheran Bible Companion*, vol. 2, edited by Edward A. Engelbrecht (St. Louis, MO: Concordia Publishing House, 2014), 971.

4 R. J. Grunewald, *Reading Romans with Luther* (St. Louis, MO: Concordia Publishing House, 2016), 101.

5 Charles Spurgeon, "Psalm 139 by C. H. Spurgeon," Blue Letter Bible, last modified December 5, 2016, https://www.blueletterbible.org /Comm/spurgeon_charles/tod/ps139.cfm.

6 *Luther's Works*, American Edition, vol. 3, edited by Jaroslav Pelikan (St. Louis, MO: Concordia Publishing House, 1961), 80.

7 *The Lutheran Study Bible* (*TLSB*) (St. Louis, MO: Concordia Publishing House, 2009), study note on Genesis 17:10.

8 *TLSB*, study note on Colossians 2:12.

9 *Lutheran Bible Companion*, vol. 2, 954.

10 Adapted from Katie Koplin, "Girl, When you wash your face, Remember your Baptism," October 31, 2018, Loved in Spite of Self, https://lovedin-spiteofself.com/2018/10/31/girl-when-you-wash-your -face-remember-your-baptism/. Used by permission.

11 Jan Johnson and Matt Rhodes, "Trusting God Retreat."

12 *Lutheran Service Book* (*LSB*) 611:1–2.

13 *Luther's Small Catechism with Explanation*, 11.

14 Charles Spurgeon, "Psalm 23 by C. H. Spurgeon," Blue Letter Bible, last Modified December 5, 2016, https://www.blueletterbible.org /Comm/spurgeon_charles/tod/ps023.cfm.

15 Grunewald, *Reading Romans with Luther*, 25.

16 *LSB* 709.